0/05

3000 800059 508
St. Louis Community College

D1238242

Meramec Library
St. Louis Community College
11333 Biq Bend Blvd.
Kirkwood, MO 63122-5799
314-984-7797

WITHDRAWN

WITHDRAWN

Dress and globalisation

Published in our
centenary year
~ **2004** ~
MANCHESTER
UNIVERSITY
PRESS

St. Louis Community College
at Meramec
LIBRARY

STUDIES IN DESIGN

general editor:
CHRISTOPHER BREWARD

founding editor:
PAUL GREENHALGH

St. Louis Community College
at Meramec
LIBRARY

Dress and globalisation

Margaret Maynard

Manchester University Press

Manchester and New York

distributed exclusively in the USA by Palgrave

Copyright © Margaret Maynard 2004

The right of Margaret Maynard to be identified as the author of this work has been asserted by her in accordance with the Copyright, Designs and Patents Act 1988.

Published by Manchester University Press
Oxford Road, Manchester M13 9NR, UK
and Room 400, 175 Fifth Avenue, New York, NY 10010, USA
www.manchesteruniversitypress.co.uk

Distributed exclusively in the USA by
Palgrave, 175 Fifth Avenue, New York, NY 10010, USA

Distributed exclusively in Canada by
UBC Press, University of British Columbia, 2029 West Mall, Vancouver, BC, Canada V6T 1Z2

British Library Cataloguing-in-Publication Data
A catalogue record for this book is available from the British Library

Library of Congress Cataloging-in-Publication Data applied for

ISBN   0 7190 6388 4 hardback
        0 7190 6389 2 paperback

First published 2004

12 11 10 09 08 07 06 05 04   10 9 8 7 6 5 4 3 2 1

Typeset in ITC Giovanni
by Carnegie Publishing, Lancaster
Printed in Great Britain
by Bell & Bain Limited, Glasgow

Before I used to dress always in a gallabiyya; now I am forced to be dressed in a suit, but from time to time I dress in my baladi-gallabiyya (native gown) and when I do so, I feel as if I am in paradise. (Statement by a Cairo-born man in 1978, quoted in Spring and Hudson, 1995).

Contents

Illustrations

Acknowledgements

I would like to thank all the following people who have generously assisted me, in various ways, in bringing this project to completion. First of all I wish to acknowledge Professor Graeme Turner, Director of the Centre for Critical and Cultural Studies, The University of Queensland, for his ongoing encouragement, and my gratitude to the Centre for a Visiting Fellowship in 2001. I must also thank Winchester School of Art, Southampton University, for a Visiting Scholarship in 2001, as well as the ARC for a small grant, funding a study of Australia and Globalisation. Carmen Luke assisted with mentorship at the University of Queensland, in the early stages of the project. As always I acknowledge Michael Carter for his continuing and generous interest and Lou Taylor for her warm encouragement of my work. Others I must thank include Glynis Jones, the Powerhouse Museum, Sydney; Karen Finch, former Director of the Textile Conservation Centre, UK; and Philip A. Sykas, Research Fellow, Manchester Metropolitan University; Sean Rintel and Amanda Taylor for research assistance; Katrina Finch ITN News, London, for help with picture research; and staff of the Muslim College, Ealing, London, for their assistance in understanding Muslim dress. My gratitude also goes to Barbara Burman and Tom Gardner for warm hospitality in London and their intellectual stimulation; Deirdre Wood for use of her illustrations taken in Mali; Mike Barnett for use of his photographs taken in South America; as well as John Pilkington, Hazel Clark and Piera Chen for permission to use their photographs. I would like to acknowledge Clare Rose for her invaluable ideas and information on ethnic dress; the detailed information personally supplied by the High Commissioner for Zambia; Birgit Culloty's skill in tracking down invaluable reference material; Antonia Finnane, University of Melbourne, and Louise Beynon, School of African and Oriental Studies for information on dress in China; and Andrea Mitchell for her technical advice. Finally I would like to thank Richard Maynard for his encouragement and unfailing support for what I do.

Introduction

Matt Dawson, 24, London. *Where do you get your clothes from?* Well I work in a second-hand vintage clothes place, and that's where I get a lot of them. This Motley Crüe T-shirt came through the shop. *What are your clothes saying today?* That I'm a second-hand boy. Mind you, I might go and take this belt back. It's doing me no good at all. (Thomas and Arora 2000)

M ATT DAWSON, in a skimpy Motley Crüe T-shirt and retro slit jeans, was one of a group of young adults in Tokyo and London interviewed about their dress by *The Face* magazine in 2000. Although living in urban cultures at opposite ends of the earth, interviewees of both sexes gave remarkably similar responses to questions about their appearances. Nonchalant and relaxed about mixing an eclectic range of styles and accessories, many had chosen borrowed or secondhand gear. Fashion for them was something likely to change weekly as part of particular activities, momentary fads and lifestyle choices. What is perhaps most marked is the degree to which they were self-conscious about their selection of down beat 'looks'. These were global consumers and they knew exactly what would best express their identity and what messages their belts, ties and shoes were intended to convey (Thomas and Arora 2000: 205–10). One question that arises is how can we meaningfully compare the current obsession with self-image in affluent countries, with many parts of the less developed world including India, Africa and Indonesia where the clothing may be very different? An example might be these Muslims at Dacca, Bangladesh clinging here to an over crowded pilgrim train, shown in Figure 1. They are dressed in a complicated mix of western style jeans, shirts, pullovers and baseball caps, but also customary knee-length *shirvani* coats and *tupa* (caps) and wrapped *lungi*, or perhaps *dhoti*.[1]

There is an added complication in global dress. Aside from the fragmentation of tastes in the west, and various permutations of ethnicity found all over the world, the clothing of professional classes who work

1 Pilgrims near Dacca, Bangladesh *c.* 1996, wearing a varied mixture of western style clothes and headwear, as well as customary attire

in fast-paced urban environments like central Shanghai, Hong Kong, New York, Sydney or Singapore occupies a further register of dressing. Favouring elegant tailored styles, purchased from designer wear stores and high-class retail chains, the attire of such men and women allows them to move freely across geographical and cultural borders. These many variables seem at odds with the commonplace assumption that we are gradually and almost inevitably succumbing to the pervasive, featureless influence of mass-produced US style clothing. Together these examples constitute the challenge posed by this book, that is to analyse and make sense of stylistic similarities, as well as widespread cultural and ethnic disparities of dress, throughout the world.

Firstly, what is globalisation? Does it embrace a defined set of practices? Is it an easy rhetorical catchall or is it largely an imagined set of perceptions about a particular historical moment? Although controversial and much debated as a concept, globalisation, for the purposes of this book will be taken to have commenced with the world crises of 1968–71, and the slowing down of overall world economic growth. The period under discussion covers the collapse of Sovietism; the consumer revolution in China; the speculative booms in equity and property markets of the 1980s; the vast social changes brought about by postcolonial rule and the changing, flexible rhythms of post Fordist production and outsourcing; the rise of multinational corporations; the globalisation of finance systems; and not least the growth of world media networks and the e-revolution. Globalisation will be taken to refer both to the condition and the rhetoric of being part of a supposedly single interwoven macro-culture, as well as the actual processes by which commodities move across the world (du Gay *et al.* 1997: 72). Even so, it must be emphasised that the interconnectedness of the First and Third Worlds, implied by the term, has taken place on unequal terms, thus making globalisation seem largely synonymous with westernisation (Wassmann 1998: 3).

What exactly do we mean by western clothing and how pervasive is its influence? Has the deterritorialised world of global marketing destroyed individual identity or does dress continue to mark our social belonging to groups constituted by class, race, ethnicity and gender? Can dress signal disaffection with political processes, and be a form of resistance to globalisation itself? And what happens to any sense of difference when clothing commodities cross over their geographical borders of origin, so that the culture they substantiate is no longer the culture in which they circulate (Howes 1996: 2)? Given the huge shifts in social habits that modern industrial society has caused, how painful and problematic for indigenous peoples is the process of self-modernisation, inevitably including changes in clothing habits? Answering these questions is, without doubt, a complicated and certainly an ambitious task.

One thing we can safely say is that all clothes are, to a degree, a form of informational exchange. Alison Lurie claims that clothing and comportment is a sign system, literally a language, with its own specific words and sentences (Lurie 1992: 4). But are clothes the precise markers of status, region, sexuality, class, ethnicity and gender that she seems to believe? In any form of encounter, especially cross-cultural engagements, dress is likely to be interpreted more obtusely than directly. The lived and subjective experience of dress, its embodied messages and its aesthetics form a more complicated material social practice than a language system. Choice of garments can often be more subtle and imprecise than vocabulary. Perhaps more significant for our purposes are the ways one social group responds in their dressing towards another, as both negotiate the pressures of the new global order. So this book examines more than the obvious language of clothing in a complex, fragmented world. It considers dress at a more symbolic level of indication, as a manifestation of the variable, sometimes contradictory social tactics of individuals and groups as they seek advantage and register their momentary place in the world (Baudrillard 1981: 36).[2]

The aim of this text is not merely to account for the ways contemporary global consumption and choice of clothing signal individual or group identity and status, although this is important. Rather, it attempts to analyse how, given income limitations, choice is also conditioned by what is offered for selection, both by a retail industry reaching out to the global, but also by more localised practices of selling, including recycling and the secondhand market. The central proposition is that, whether we are talking about the developed or the underdeveloped world, consumers make in-formed and strategic decisions about what they wear. Within a global framework mass-produced clothing, whatever its origin, cannot simply be regarded as homogenous. It can be chosen and worn in a great variety of individual, sometimes ambiguous ways, thus challenging any notion of formalised or regularised dress coding.

Hansen, in her important studies of African dress and dynamic trans-national flows of used clothing, shows that in Zambian secondhand street markets, consumers pick and choose from amongst the used goods on offer, to find 'new' outfits that best suit their self-image. This used clothing is termed *salaula*, meaning in the Bemba language 'to select from a pile', or *kaunjika*, which means to 'pick' in Nyanja (Hansen 1994: 506). In Tanzania it is called *kafa ulaya* – that is 'Died in Europe' (Weiss 1996: 138). Hansen demonstrates how Zambian consumers are discriminating in their choice of goods, sometimes pulling clothes apart and resewing or altering them, and then wearing them in ways that suit their own bodies, both physically and culturally. A similar practice occurs in West Africa with the *fuug jaay* tailors. They specifically alter secondhand imported clothing, such as suits, reconfiguring them with trims and badges for local tastes and in defiance of the status quo (Mustafa 1998: 31). This renders the wearers 'Zambian' or 'West African', primarily through the act of selection or modification of their attire. Hansen shows that the only thing western about western clothes in Zambia is their origin and imprint (Hansen 1999: 14). Thus it is consumers who bring meaning to bear on their choice of clothing. Equally interesting is the fact that western clothing, often originally made in third world countries, is then exported back there as secondhand goods creating a complex cycle of meaningfulness and biographical com-plexity (Hansen 1995: 278).

If western dress becomes Zambian, Nigerian or anything else by the fact of its wearing or remaking, it must surely undermine the whole concept of cultural style as discrete. On one level this makes African consumers little different from young people like Matt Dawson, who pick and choose from secondhand goods, although their economic circumstances differ widely. Choice of what to wear is, of course, never unlimited, except for those few without economic constraints. Selection is always made from a repertoire of social and economic possibilities, or a culturally defined suite of goods, and it is the tactics and strategies of wearing, within variants of social repertoire, that are of interest here. At the extreme base line of cultures, clothing is worn primarily for covering and warmth, as with charity clothing. However, as soon as it is economically possible to make a choice, the choice becomes significant and thus advantageous. As Emma Tarlo argues in her groundbreaking study of dress in India, civilian clothing behaviour is socially prescribed, yet at the same time not absolutely determined at all. She suggests that people themselves abide by classifications but these are open to dispute and alternation. So to a significant degree they are able to choose their own identities. Clothes are products, but they are also products in use. So clothes don't just inform, people use them tactically to define, to present, to communicate, to deceive, to play with and so on (Tarlo 1996: 7–8). They are central to identity but not in a deterministic way.

When choice is an option for consumers, it is inevitably made in relation to their notions of cultural identity, although, as Daniel Miller advises, making causal links between consumption and identity is unwise (Miller 1995: 34). This connection with culture is implicit in everyday urban dressing as in subculture and 'ethnic' clothing. Assuming a capacity for choice exists, then the process of identity formation can never be static, and it becomes impossible to regard identity as fully definable or stable. Representing the self is ambivalent and often culturally unsettling (Hendrickson 1996: 5). We must therefore see cultural and personal identity as relational, even nomadic, and subject to continuous repositioning. Role-playing possibilities in cyberspace chat-rooms offer yet more choices, although these, it must be said, are available only to those fortunate enough to be inside rather than outside 'the loop of information' (Lash 1999: 344).

Despite the acknowledged degree of choice implicit in global dress, the wearing of westernised, secondhand or even locally made replicas of western clothing is so widespread it is found in the most remote parts of the globe, be it Africa, Asia or South America. It is important to note that for a range of cultural reasons, some under discussion in this book, women have generally been slower to adopt western style dress than men. In this image of a festival at Antigua in Guatemala, Mayan men wear fully western style dress. The young boy in jeans and NY logo baseball cap is indistinguishable from someone living in the US or Europe, although the reasons why he wears what he wears are likely to be quite different from boys in the US. By comparison the women have retained their brightly coloured customary styles and thus their ethnic links (Figure 2).[3] But the perception, and to a degree the fact of, homogenisation in dress, apparently evident in say the clothing of Guatemalan men, may be misleading. Theorists and historians like Appadurai (1996), Howes (1996), Mathews (2000) and Schoss (1996) question the very notion of the US as monolithic controller of values and commodities, pointing to localised tastes and identities. Despite the speed of cultural information transfer, the new possibilities engendered by travel and the diasporic spread of communities means geographical borders are ever shifting. Indeed in a close study of cosmo-politan styles of dress and behaviour adopted by locals in the East African coastal town of Malindi between 1989–91, Schoss found that transnational contact laid the ground not for one homogenised identity but for a 'multiplicity of cosmopolitanisms' (Schoss 1996: 184), all of which existed alongside local dress. So boundaries between subjects, cultural, economic and ethnic groups and clans, are undergoing constant reformulation, countering any notion of uniformity in clothes as well as art, entertainment, food and so on.

Appadurai has theorised about these complications in his text *Modernity at Large*. In this account he examines the conditions in which global flows occur. They happen, in his view, in and through imaginary models or 'scapes' (Appadurai 1996: 37). These are made up of complex and profound disjunctures between homogeneity and heterogeneity in the economy, culture and politics, each inflected by social differences and perspectives.

2 Mayan men at Antigua in 1995, in western style dress, the women in brightly coloured 'ethnic' garments

3 Crowds of men at a cattle market, Ayorou village, Niger 2003. The dress is a complex mix of capacious *boubou* robes, turban-like *chéche* and western style clothing

He comes to the conclusion that these global flows create a form of cultural chaos that partly accounts for some of the uneasy overlaps in clothing styles occurring between relative social stability and communities in motion.

The late twentieth and early twenty-first centuries have seen the political intensification of sectarianism, in terms of nationalism, indigenous self-determination and ethnicity, often using dress to affirm social, cultural and political identities. In some parts of the world, international cosmo-politan dress is scarcely worn. But 'ethnic' and customary dress itself is a fluid concept and can be subject to fashionable changes of various kinds. Moreover, in countries like Egypt, Indonesia, Africa and India, customary and western dress are frequently alternated on a daily basis or worn by people concurrently. This view of a cattle market at Ayorou village, Niger (Figure 3) shows some attendees in customary *boubou* and *chéche* head-dresses, whilst others wear western style jackets, shirts and trousers. In many places western encroachment on traditional or 'ethnic' dress has not been straightforward and western dress is not necessarily accepted without question. It may be rejected, or else complex cultural entanglements can take place between the specialities of region and the intrusion of the global.

This happens in cultural practices beyond clothing, since there are versions of the English language spoken in Ghana, Nigeria and Singapore that are largely unintelligible to other English speakers.

Consumption of dress can be a form of creolisation, where nothing is dominant and nothing is entirely traditional, resulting in hybrid dress forms. But even the term creolisation, or cultural chaos, seems to mis-represent some dress practices. It implies an undifferentiated form of mixture that can misread the partial assumption of clothing or the tactical, strategic or even sheer inventiveness of some global dressing. For instance in Guatemalan villages women, who can be wearing their local customary dress, sometimes drape western style cardigans on their heads, so that it is western garments that closely replicate indigenous folded headwear (Herald 1992: 130). This is indicative of the way traditional dress is not a fixed entity but signifies dress codes in which there is a constant incorporation of new ideas. It supports Taylor's argument that there has never been a fully uncontaminated 'authenticity' either in peasant or in 'tribal' dress (Taylor 2002: 201–5). Therefore what we mean by western, or indeed 'ethnic' clothing, is sometimes hard to define with any degree of precision. In fact, instead of a generalised, progressive capitulation to the force of the American way of life, Friedman (1994) and Appadurai (1996) offer analytical models that can be used to show ways in which we can detect all types of conscious cultural resistances, as well as group and individual choices and preferences that suggest something more unequal.[4] This might parallel what some see as the different order of articulation between global systems; between say the US and Japan, compared to Tanzania or Bangladesh (Holton 1998: 202).

So, in any account of global clothing we need to accept the universal ubiquity of the baseball cap, jeans, skirts and blouses and trainers (although even here meanings can have local resonances). But we also need to account for the continued wearing of such garments as the Indonesian *peci* cap, the Muslim *hijab* and the Indian sari. We need to be able to explain the Japanese taste for the business suit, their proclivity for the white wedding rather than the Shinto wedding,[5] and even the appropriation of the Indian Nehru jacket by European haute couture. We need to account for subsets of these clothing practices and acknowledge the sometimes subtle markers of caste, class, gender, age, cultural identity and individuality as people constantly negotiate their place in a changing world.

A study of global dress must consider clothing in its broadest sense, rather than confine discussion to the upper end of the fashion market. Given the discrepancies between rich and poor nations, and the complex-ities of globalisation and of advanced capitalism in the late twentieth and early twenty-first centuries, high fashion (which itself may have subsets) is most often about extreme forms of glamour, celebrity status, the media and catwalk performance. Some might even argue that fashion is more virtual than real, with the exception perhaps of a small minority who can afford haute couture. Even more than this, it would seem that status distinction in many parts of the developed world can be less about what you wear and more about what time you can afford, or the latest technology. Yet status is communicated differently in various parts of the world, for instance in the People's Republic of the Congo, prior to the 1997 revolution, where acquisition of French couture was deemed the ultimate status symbol for the underclass *Sapeurs* (see chapter 1), rather than for the elite.

The domination of global clothing companies, while a powerful factor in current consumption is by no means absolute. Ostensibly western products are continually being recreated around the world from the local perspective (Howes 1996: 190). Although diffusion of US style goods still presents non-westerners with dilemmas, consumers even in newly developing countries at the start of the twenty-first century are regarded as having far greater agency in the construction of their own personal identity than previously (Howes 1996: 179). Importantly, in a global landscape, where goods are widely transported across national and cultural boundaries, dress meanings do not necessarily speak univocally or to a single audience, but are widely and variously decoded from one culture to the next. To understand global dressing then is to see that clothing has no discrete or intrinsic meaning.

Methodology

This project initially grew out of a dissatisfaction with certain kinds of Eurocentric dress and fashion histories, the limitations implicit in some linear histories of period style, and accounts of dress as a fairly straight-forward conveyor of social meaning, class and hierarchy. Although written from a western perspective, it is offered partly as a critique of some dress or fashion studies preoccupied with western style as dominant, or presuming to speak on behalf of other cultures. These earlier studies include economic models of dressing as stylistic novelty, prestige and status competition (Veblen 1934), or the conceptualisation of dress as a decodable sign system or form of communication embedded in textual discourse (Barthes 1983; Lurie 1992; and Barnard 1996).

This having been said, one must acknowledge that since the mid-1990s the ground of dress studies shifted dramatically. Changes have come about largely as a result of the intervention of feminist scholars and anthropologists, the impact of cultural and media studies, the study of material culture, and the importance placed on studies of consumption. This historiography and the methodological spread of dress and fashion studies is comprehensively discussed by Lou Taylor in her important work *The Study of Dress History*, 2002.[6] In addition, since its inception in 1997, crucial new work has regularly appeared in the journal *Fashion Theory*, which has acted as a forum for new theoretical approaches to dress. Nor should we overlook the innovative approach of scholars like Christopher Breward, who was instrumental in introducing methods that straddle a number of areas including cultural studies, economics, as well as design and art history (Breward 1995). Finally we must acknowledge as well that dress history is increasingly being written by those who can speak on behalf of, or from the position of those beyond a dominant white mainstream (Puwar 2002; Franklin 2001).

Within the new climate of dress studies, Jennifer Craik has recently, and very usefully, argued that fashion is a phenomenon that is not unique to western capitalism and that we must reassess our notion that fashion is purely an elite practice. She also advises that we obliterate distinctions between western and non-western systems of style, reconstituting them as sets of competing systems or technologies, encompassing everyday and more exclusive practices. This approach, which she defines as a study of the techniques of civility or the constitution of the social habitus, lies well beyond mere clothes and encompasses gestures, dispositions, comportment and so on (Craik 1994: 4). While fully endorsing Craik's proposition that there are many systems of dress operating in some form of relation one to another, this present study prefers to regard fashion as those clothes of the elite that embody the latest, most desirable aesthetic codes, in addition to being one of many competing systems. In developing the case that dress is not always a matter of competing systems, this book shows that choice of what to wear can take place outside this form of practice, as in 'alternative' clothing which can be said to occupy a different register, rather than a competing one.

In the course of establishing the methodology used in this book, I must gratefully acknowledge prior work undertaken on aspects of global dress and difference by Joanne Eicher and colleagues in *Dress and Ethnicity* (1995) and *The Visible Self* (2000). In both works, Eicher *et al.* argue for the generalised term 'world dress' to be applied to what is regarded as commonly worn clothing (Eicher and Sumberg 1995: 296; Eicher *et al.* 2000: 46). This is defined as shirts, suits, and so on, worn for urban employment and for international events (Eicher *et al.* 2000: 253). At the same time Eicher's studies fully acknowledge the importance of 'ethnic' and national traits in attire, as well as the fact that western dress has been shown to mutate in places like India, the Philippines and Africa. She also accepts that the trend toward homogenisation can blind us to those forms of clothing which exist beyond the appearance of ostensible sharing (255). So her books are important precursors to this present study, for she accepts the important social needs and pleasures implicit in 'difference', within global patterns of consumption.

I am especially indebted to one essay in *Dress and Ethnicity*, concerned with the dress of Highland Indians in Ecuador, by anthropologist Carola Lentz between 1983 and 1985. This considers, and attends usefully to identifying, the multiplicity of meanings implicit in changing dress codes of Indian migrant workers on the coast, who seek to avoid ethnic discrimination by adopting, and indeed retaining, aspects of western dress as their own. Lentz discusses the attendant complexities of these dress strategies, variously adopted by both men and women, as part of redefining traditional Indian culture and restructuring Indian mestizo relationships (Lentz 1995: 289). I acknowledge as well the important text *Clothing and Difference* (1996), edited by Hendrickson, with its series of essays that focus on aspects of African dress, and its complex often ambivalent meanings as bodily inscription.

So this is a study of relational practices of dress and bodily adornment. Taking in part from the theories of De Certeau in *The Practice of Everyday Life* (1984), this book examines the dress of globally dominant cultures but in relation to what he regards as the socially marginal majority. Although De Certeau does not consider the subject of dress, I wish to apply some of his ideas to clothing, which will demonstrate quite cogently the kinds of social struggles that are part of his concern. This book also accepts Baudrillard's analysis of the symbolic social logic and strategies used by groups and individuals to their own social advantage, often overriding the use value of objects, in this case clothing (Baudrillard 1981). By using the concept of a separation between privileged, dominant social groups and their systems, and the ruses or insinuations of the 'other', chiefly non-privileged groups, this book offers an enmeshed account of style, acknowledging the ongoing interchanges and style resistances that take place in social encountering. It also takes the view that we are all engaged in complex and shifting processes of self-presentation, crucial to the creation of personal but also national, ethnic and international identities.

Given the paradoxes, fragmentation and lack of consensus, in the 'network society', the intention is to consider apparently generic types of clothing, suits and trainers, but in proximity and sometimes antagonism to examples of many counter discourses of 'difference'. Here the issue of dress terminology is clearly fraught with complications. Building partly on Eicher's definitions in *The Visible Self*, I use the term western throughout this book fairly loosely to describe clothing whose style, if not its making, originates in the industrial world of Europe and America. This clothing is constantly in some form of relationship with other kinds of dress, and may indeed be an ingredient in hybrid or bicultural clothing. The clothing of 'difference' that constitutes a counterpoint to western style, defined above, includes customary or 'ethnic' dress, that is attire characteristic of a specific language, religious and ethnographic social group and may be worn by diasporic peoples who retain allegiance to their cultural heritage (Eicher *et al.* 2000: 36). The term 'ethnic' is preferred to traditional, which implies a form of unchanging attire. There is also the case that 'ethnic' features may be used to construct self-consciously national dress on the part of the state, or itself have region specific inflections. The term will also necessarily encompass clothes worn by say those of African heritage, living outside their countries of origin, and where links to a special ethnographic social group or language no longer exist.

The term 'ethnic' clothing is sometimes described as peasant dress. Unfortunately this sometimes has pejorative associations, although it can have a place in describing social groups with links to an agricultural existence. Then there is provincial dress and small-scale community dress, which may be inflected by location or particularly regional proclivities,[7] subcultural clothing (characterised here as a subset of urban dress), and 'new age' attire, all of which are used as terms but subject to a host of variable manifestations. The important general point is that we need to be wary of setting up false dichotomies between western style dress and the dress of 'others', between supposedly homogenous western dress and for example the clothes of Muslims in countries like Iran and Afghanistan or local customary dress in Africa or Romania. So what is considered here are the tensions, effects or differences that are set up, as well as the political and class tactics that are engaged upon and played out as part of ongoing and changing relationships between international clothing and local style. The former can be global styles or branded products manufactured by companies like Nike and Benetton, or styles that may not be so visible, defined rather by their blandness. And local styles may be ethnic attire, or may be a further hybrid construct of some kind, making use of national, regional, political or religious clothing signifiers. Nor should we forget the large part played by exoticised ethnicity as it is appropriated by the west and diverted into cutting edge global fashion design (Puwar 2002: 64)

Initially this study was divided into two parts. The first was intended to explore the internationalisation of both the consumption and production of clothing, raising the issue of 'sameness' as a factor of global dressing. Part two was structured as a counterpoint to the first part. Here I hoped to use a number of case studies to examine national, regional and local responses to the global. But as the study progressed, it became evident that such an artificial separation could not comprehend the complex and variable entanglements and interweavings we find in global clothing.

Instead, this book looks widely, and in an overarching sense, at the ways in which cultures interact and engage with each other at the level of appearance. What we find is shifting, often uneven, patterns of consumption expressed in the garments we wear, our hair, headwear and our beautification, all taking place as consumers come to terms with a new world order. Accepting there are pitfalls in a study of this magnitude, there are also worthwhile issues to confront in the process of grappling with the range of source materials. My gratitude is extended to those who have undertaken many specifically localised and specialised studies of dress, many groundbreaking, upon which I have frequently drawn. As a project this can only commence the process of understanding current clothing styles. At the same time it represents a search for a new approach to the subject of dress. It draws together the threads of studies of consumption, ethnicity, gender and the body, as well as studies of representation, that is intended to be sensitive to the voices of lower socio-economic groups. The chapters include accounts of the importance of headwear and hairdressing, the issue of consuming so called 'ethnic chic', clothes for the tourist market, the politicisation of traditional dress by world leaders, 'alternative' dressing, and the wearing of T-shirts as temporary markers of identity. The final chapter considers dress and environmental issues, touching on adventure gear, the 'green' consumer and the possible impact of 'smart' clothing. As its overarching intention, this book specifically examines the ways in which clothing is engendered to signify social and national identity. It analyses how different categories of consumer relate to each other through the materials and symbolism of their clothing, and how relationships are altered and transformed by this engagement. First and foremost it asks the question, how do the meanings of dress ebb and flow in the process of social encountering?

Notes

1 *Lungi* are cotton cloths worn around the waist that are sewn into shape, while *dhoti* are unsewn.

2 My thanks to Rex Butler for drawing my attention to the relevance of this text.

3 Eicher *et al.* (2000: 204) suggest that the state in Guatemala distrusts adherence to 'ethnic' Indian dress, seeing it as symptomatic of political unrest, even revolution.

4 For some, Americanisation and westernisation are synonymous. This may be debatable but is not an issue that affects the propositions of this book.

5 Christian white weddings in Japan are considered to be cheaper and more relaxed than a traditional Shinto wedding, with kimono and complicated hairstyle, *Observer Magazine* 1999: 7.

6 Entwistle's chapter 'Theorising Fashion and Dress' in *The Fashioned Body*, 2000a, is also a useful summary of theories of dress and fashion to date.

7 Eicher offers the example of the variety of provincial dress in Sweden and the Amish who share a communal ideology but whose dress varies regionally (2000: 107, 250).

1 ✦ Theorising global dress

> The truth is I am a pretty fun guy. Most people don't know it but I like
> to salsa a great deal and have an outstanding collection of bow ties that
> I have been building up for many years. Every time I go overseas I try
> to buy a new one … no one wants to be seen out with Jacques
> [Derrida] because, well, he still wears those hideous brown suits with
> beige ties. That's Paris for you. (Jean Baudrillard in an interview with
> Benjamin Genocchio, *Australian's Review of Books* 2001)

GLOBALISATION has become a contemporary fact of life. All of us,
whether we live in Europe, Africa, South America or the Philippines,
are caught up in a vast network of transnational relations and
interlinked patterns of consumption. Yet globalisation is a most inexact
term and its time frame is debatable. The very nature of globalisation
seems to work against any form of consensual meaning (Childs and
Williams 1997: 213). But for current purposes let us consider it as
encompassing the ongoing and imprecise array of dramatic and transforming international changes in politics, the media, business, health, new
technologies, manufacturing methods and consumption occurring since the
1970s. Opinions about its benefits vary widely. Much depends on where
one lives, one's current educational and economic status and one's future
prospects. There are those who are deeply concerned about its effects,
fearing the stateless alliances of capital and power, as well as the production
methods and market integration of huge multinational corporations. Yet
many applaud its evident benefits. They point to technological innovations,
enlarged communications networks, advancements in health services, the
freeing up of trade and commerce, and of course increased possibilities
for personal mobility, itself engendering and intensifying cultural and
commercial exchanges, borrowings and adaptations. For the financially
privileged the world seems increasingly to merge into a single entity but
in other terms it often seems to be falling apart (Wassmann 1998: 4).

In a world where social and economic differences are endemic, where the most pressing contemporary concerns are global warming, refugee and migration problems, the HIV Aids epidemic, food shortages, pollution and unemployment, dress might seem an insignificant aspect of life. Yet this is certainly not the case. For instance, the textile and apparel industries are the largest source of industrial employment in the world (Dickerson 1999: 5). Such manufacturing is of unparalleled significance in developing countries. In 1996 apparel was the tenth largest world trade category (Dickerson 1999: 183). Dickerson shows that in 1999, of an estimated two hundred nations in the world, virtually all of them produced apparel and textiles, and, to varying degrees, contributed to the world clothing market (Dickerson 1999: 46). Some of these countries, Bangladesh and Sri Lanka for instance, are actually economically dependent on this trade. So we must accept that clothing production and consumption is a crucial factor within the global environment, and that dress is important in a variety of ways to all peoples, whatever their income level. Indeed in most cultures one acquires social authenticity by what one wears. So to study dress, its production, distribution methods and disparate patterns of consumption, is to go to the heart of understanding the shaping of self and identity within a global framework. This applies to western nations, just as much as to their neighbours in the third and fourth world.[1]

Given that apparel is so significant, not just in terms of framing and asserting identity but also to economic prosperity, can a study of dress and its practices help to explain wider social and political issues within the global landscape? How, for instance, does dress relate to authentication of social categories, the legitimating and contesting of authority, engagements of class, the demarcation of age and gender, the formulation and performance of identity, the definition of nation and/or race, and in what ways is it implicated in political strategies? This chapter highlights some of the paradoxes of appearance and identity in the modern world. A number of theoretical texts that deal with globalisation can assist in an attempt to come to terms with these uneasy and often uneven overlaps between clothing in the developed world and the partial retention, and/or recreation of customary dress, in less developed nations. A fundamental question is whether the differences between metropolitan dressing, rural and provincial dressing and of course 'ethnic' style are being wiped out in favour of a generalised Americanisation of appearance, a set of practices that Eicher and Sumberg term 'world' or 'cosmopolitan' fashion (Eicher and Sumberg 1995: 296). In this respect, theoretical approaches to globalisation can throw useful light on current usage of clothing. What seems to be the case is that there appears to be less a form of 'world' attire, than a simultaneous articulation of global homogeneity together with an emphasis on many subsets of local or tactical 'difference'.

In order to appreciate the nature of our topic, we need first to have some brief understanding of the social and political period under consideration. The years immediately after 1968 saw a crisis of confidence in the western political process. This was accelerated in the US by the assassinations of Martin Luther King and Robert Kennedy, and student riots in Europe and elsewhere. Among factors causing fundamental changes to the world's geographical and political boundaries were the oil crisis and price hike, leading to a US recession in 1974–75, the Iranian Revolution in 1979, the disintegration of the Cold War in the 1980s, the invasion of Kuwait by Saddam Hussein in 1990, and the final collapse of the Soviet Union in 1991. At the same time the dismantling of colonialism was made manifest in many African countries like South Africa. Yugoslavia splintered into segments, as did the former Soviet Union, becoming eventually fifteen separate states. By contrast the European Union, formed in 1993, is a co-operative grouping with the number of full member countries still growing. Throughout this period we see the expanding influence of vast multinational corporations, the pervasive influence of the media, including Hollywood with its particular brand of consumerism, all affecting attitudes to dress in one way or another. Jameson regards this almost unchallenged encroachment of economic and cultural influence to be a malign force which he terms the 'American way of life'; the only apparent alternative being religious fundamentalism (Jameson 1999: 64). Although strangely prophetic given the events of 2001, this seems to assume an extreme polarity between west and east, even centre and periphery. This is something not fully borne out in detail, either in terms of ethnic diversity or related dress practices around the world, and of course many multinational companies generate ideas and products from outside of the US.

Nearly three-quarters of the world's larger countries are not culturally homogeneous but have politically significant minorities. This was made especially evident by extreme ethnic and nationalist conflicts in Africa and Eurasia that accelerated in the early 1990s (Kegley and Wittkopf 2001a: 173–5). While the upsurge in robust nationalism and strengthening of local cultures in the 1980s and 1990s was partly the express result of globalisation, there has been, at the same time, a cultural fragmentation and widespread search for new and further expressions of identity. Friedman attributes this pluralism to a loss of faith in capitalist homogenisation, mass culture and the progress of 'civilisation' itself (Friedman 1994: 78–80). So in addition to the growing Americanisation of world culture, together with quests for self-identity in the west by some minority groups, elsewhere there has been a weakening of former nationalist identities and the emergence of new alliances. These have been not so much based on citizenship, or even loyalty to the nation state, but on other primordial loyalties of ethnicity, local community and language (Friedman 1994: 86). At the same time, since the 1970s, there has been a widespread experience of diaspora, resulting in the replacement of centralism with concomitant forms of social diversity. Vast movements of people away from their country of origin have taken place, especially away from underdeveloped nations, both as migrants and refugees. By the 1980s, according to Sowell's estimate, 50–55 million people were living outside their land of birth, 60 per cent coming from less developed countries (Sowell 1994: 37). Today this number of displaced or replaced persons has risen almost threefold. In addition, in 1998 more than 22 million people qualified and received refugee assistance (Kegley and Wittkopf 2001b: 303). We may consider these people as large groupings, Lebanese, Filipino and so on, but such groups may themselves be thinking and acting, often dressing, in smaller particular ways and entities, thus signalling further alliances or animosities.

Within the instability of the postmodern world, a world in which there appears to be less and less social, ethical or political agreement, the nature and extent of global homogenisation of clothing is both evident but also unclear. The picture we have is one whose dimensions alter with great rapidity. Extreme variants between the rich and poor are daily reported in the press. Yet data contained in the World Bank's 2001 report *Income Net – Income Poverty*, suggests that in the 1990s poverty declined in rapidly growing countries but increased in countries that experienced stagnation or drought.[2] This report contains comparative statistics suggesting that in the developing countries the share of the population living on less than US$1 a day actually fell from 28 per cent in 1987 to 23 per cent in 1998. A similar reduction occurred in those living on less than US$2 a day. What is clear from World Bank data is that it is impossible to generalise about income and poverty levels from country to country, and within countries between rural and urban populations. All of these geographical, economic and social differences complicate the ways in which individuals and social groups respond to the supposed domination of western clothing. In the final analysis it is impossible to offer absolute or categorical views on these issues, as local tastes and habits of wearing are inflected by economic variables and are constantly shifting in response to changing social factors.

It is the present proposition that dress is caught up in fundamental paradoxes between global 'sameness' of appearance, and disjunctures, made up of ever shifting and incomplete processes of identity formation. These result in unceasing alterations of meaning. In complex ways appearance today is culturally managed or neglected, in accordance with particular social requirements but always subject to economic constraints. Commodities are transposed from place of production to place of consumption, and the reception of them may not have the same articulation as at the source. In Appadurai's terms, objects circulate in different regimes of space and time, acquiring meaning and new value in the process of exchange, or in the local context of wearing (Appadurai 1986: 4). Thomas, in his account of reciprocities and the ways in which the evaluation of material objects takes place across western and Pacific indigenous cultures, argues that cultural differences are never absolute. The transaction of goods is tied up in a cross-cultural network of relations and asymmetries that he usefully terms our 'mutual entanglements' (Thomas 1991: 9). If we apply this concept to dress, we see that garments may have no intrinsic meaning in themselves but are available for interpretation and reinterpretation, based on particular uses, social circumstances and social evaluation, all of which are dependent on context.

Yet, even if we are mutually 'entangled', the agency of individual choice, although socially and culturally mediated, does mean the construction of appearance is the direct result of specific decisions about identity and status, although these decisions may well be altered in the process of social encountering. The choice of individual Muslim women to wear either the *hijab*, full *purdah* or western dress, or a combination of clothing, when living in a country other than their own, provides a good example of such accommodation. In past centuries status in dress was demonstrated via socially agreed codes, bedded down in relations of class and gender. Such coded items were evident – gold ornaments, fine textiles, watches and jewellery – their use prescribed, even if not always adhered to, prior to the eighteenth century by sumptuary laws.[3] Nowadays, stylish self-fashioning in the developed world is far more individualistic, frivolous and hedonistic than before (Lipovetsky 1994: 11). Within our pluralistic and diversified world, there are no longer absolute sartorial rules (Crane 2000: 168). Clothes for the income rich are often less important as cohesive signifiers of status, except that is for a small percentage of young affluent consumers, those few who patronise high fashion, and certain youth subcultural groups. The primary demarcator of status in income rich, present day modern societies is more likely to be the technological fashionability of luxury motor cars and mobile phones.

Generally speaking, dress today is freed from its earlier class rigidities; indeed its meanings sometimes mutate across class and socio-cultural boundaries. Yet this is not to deny the significance of status in dress, even for the income poor. In the third world society of the Democratic Republic of the Congo (certainly prior to the 1997 Laurent Kabila revolution) the hyper consumption of western couture labels by poor young men, of the Brazzaville club set, was evidently a key element in the construction of social prestige, termed *Le Sape*. Often unemployed, these young men, *Les*

Sapeurs, sought to acquire French haute couture by any means possible (Friedman 1994: 158). They also took part in an elaborate urban ritual of self-definition, which included temporary moves to Paris itself. The accumulation of a Parisian wardrobe by the very lowest members of society was not merely a symbol of social position, for the practice of accumulating prestigious labels to display on their lapels signified outside 'cargo'. This strikes at the very heart of the traditional hierarchical ordering of society. A *Sapeur* was not a dandy or trickster, nor one who looked 'sharp' or smartly put together (Schoss 1996: 168–9). Rather he was someone authenticated by what he wore. Thus *Sapeurs* regarded clothes, not so much as status symbols, but actually embodying a 'life force' believed to be a conduit to their health, success and political power (Friedman 1994: 106–8).

Theories of dress and of the global

What are some of the theories of globalisation that can be applied in this study? In turn, what theories of dress and fashion should we acknowledge as significant and what are their limitations? Many theorists of dress, especially writers on fashion, agree that our current postmodern period is one where there is a flight from the univocal in attire as in other cultural practices. A number of authors regard ambivalence as a fundamental characteristic of fashion/dress in the developed world, and some see the culturally unsettling as a feature of the postmodern experience itself (Davis 1992; Kaiser *et al.* 1991; Hendrickson 1996; Wilson 1985). This understanding of the importance of ambivalence has centred mainly on fashion's paradoxical status as both bodily margin and boundary (Warwick and Cavallaro 1998: xvii). Boultwood and Jerrard suggest that the fundamentally ambiguous nature of both the body and fashion engenders a further instability between opposing factors of self and social differentiation. All of this, they believe, drives the current fashion process (Boultwood and Jerrard 2000: 317).

Kaiser *et al.* have also pursued the issue of ambiguity in some detail, arguing that our current cultural uncertainty and social fluidity parallels constant experimentation with appearance management and style (Kaiser 1991: 167–8). They suggest that if we wish to explain the troubling nature of fashion, and the uncertain 'supermarket of style', we need to link the macro level of the marketplace and the micro level of personal choice. We need to do this by means of a symbolic concept of style ambiguity (Kaiser 1991: 180). Understanding that dressing in the developed world primarily involves personal choices, they claim that in order to explain western fashion we must 'track' the changing pathways and uses of this symbolic ambiguity (Kaiser 1991: 172). The notion that we can track clothing, both materially and conceptually, is useful. But, as the authors focus solely on fashions in the developed world, the inconsistent, sometimes unequal, and certainly ever changing relationship that western clothing has with 'ethnic' or national dress is inevitably overlooked. Moreover the theory cannot account for cases where dress codes or edicts deny individual choice, as with regulations about uniform clothing. So whilst accepting ambivalence is inherent in the fashion process and indeed in much everyday attire, the global landscape of dress is far more complicated than this set of preoccupations.

Offering a more useful approach to dress as it relates to the global is Jennifer Craik's study *The Face of Fashion* (1994). She argues that western fashion is not unique, but that throughout the world there are many sets of competing systems or technologies of the body, encompassing both everyday and more exclusive practices. Fashion, she suggests, is not simply the haute couture of Paris, but consists of systems unconfined to a particular economic or cultural set of circumstances. Indeed many other fashion systems co-exist and compete with European high fashion, including those of indigenous and non-capitalist systems (Craik 1994: xi). She also argues that the relationship between 'ethnic' styles and the west are a case of dual and competing systems, between which there are inevitably 'leakages' (Craik 1994: 39). Her entire text offers an important critique of centralised European couture and its propaganda. Whilst one might quibble about her undifferentiated use of the term 'fashion' as simply a technique of acculturation, Craik's view that dress is, at times, about dual and competing technologies of the body and its clothed habits is insightful. Moreover, when she discusses the dress of non-western cultures, and their engagements with the west, her view of the complex playing off of one dress code and body technique against another comes closest to the general proposition offered here (Craik 1994: 30). But the dualities of which she speaks are frequently made up of contradictory, unequal, often strategic social exchanges, schemas and choices. These may or may not encompass the non-uniform, the syncretic, the marginal and the hybrid. So whilst agreeing with the metaphor of 'leakages', style relationships are not quite as contained as Craik maintains. They may be, but are not necessarily, systematically competitive. At the same time the counter discourse may be an ideologically resistant one, or can be merely a different register of consumption. This is the case, for instance, with African and Indian consumers of secondhand street market goods, who choose selectively from imported garments.

If we move to theories of the wider global process itself these fall, according to Jonathan Friedman, into two large categories. There are those that focus on worldwide interconnections, cultural flows and interchanges, and those he terms the global systems approach which he himself favours (Friedman 1994: 195). Seeing an encompassing relationship between global systems and the processes of globalisation, he suggests there are, within these systems, variable and dialectical articulations between 'central' sectors and peripheries (Friedman 1994: 205–6). Appadurai takes up a similar position with regard to a global system in which cultural processes occur. He conceives of the global as a series of imaginary frameworks that consist of overlapping and increasingly disjunctive and unstable flows between the economy, culture and politics. These he terms ideoscapes, technoscapes, ethnoscapes, mediascapes and financescapes, each subject to social differences and processes. These flows emerge as tensions arise between the homogenisation of culture and cultural heterogenisation. He regards these models of unstable cultural shape to be both fractal and overlapping, moving and congealing at specific points, resulting in a kind of postmodern mix or chaos. (Appadurai 1996: 40ff). If we apply this concept of disjunctive flows to dress, one might call this mixture of style a form of creolisation or hybridity where nothing is dominant, entirely traditional, or fully modern, and of which there are certainly examples.

But whilst the consumption of dress functions in ways that are always in motion, as garments shift from one usage to another, and indeed are mutated across cultures, the issue of creolisation or cultural chaos is rather more problematic. It implies a generally undifferentiated mixture or hybridity that can misrepresent the tactical or temporary intentions of some dressing. Admittedly there are certainly garments that can be described as hybrid – for example clothes especially marketed to Romanian women under Ceausescu's rule made up of 'a dose of peasant embroidery incorporated within a dash of glitzed-up Western European fashion' (Taylor 2002: 227). But there are situations where different types of clothing are put together in a more complex manner, where garments are not hybrid per se. This is demonstrated in a photograph of a Bambara man from the Mali village of Fanembougo taken in 1996 (Figure 4). In order to go hunting he is dressed in a traditional tunic of dark brown and cream Bogolanfini mud cloth, but he wears it with ragged modern shorts and sandals. His companion, though, is dressed in a shapeless internationally generic T-shirt and faded jeans, probably charity clothing or secondhand garments of some kind. For pragmatic reasons the hunter has assumed a mixture of western style and customary dress, something that one could term a tactical use of dress.

Friedman usefully argues that globalisation is more systematic than the notion of cultural chaos or even cultural entanglement. He feels that it is more a simultaneous standardisation of institutions and markets,

4 A Malian hunter in 1996.
He wears a traditional tunic
of Bogolanfini mud cloth, but
modern shorts and sandals,
possibly charity clothing or
secondhand garments

together with a fragmentation and multiplication of what he calls localising strategies (Friedman 1994: 211). In subsequent writing he talks even more vividly of 'an era of explosive identifications, indigenous, ethnic, national and regional', a process he feels is best termed balkanisation rather than creolisation (Friedman 1998: 41). This concept of local strategising would account for the combination of western and customary dress worn by the two Mali villagers where the histories and genealogies of particular dress practices need to be specifically understood.

Global processes contain and transform their own internal boundaries and engage dialectically with the local structures that together constitute them (Friedman 1994: 206). This double, yet unbalanced articulation, and increasing interconnectedness between the overarching and the local, is notoriously uneven (Wassmann 1998: 3). So a study of global dress must not only address the wealthy and fashionable and those, probably the majority, who can afford some choice of clothing, but must also consider those who simply manage to get by and others, like the Malians, who live on or below the poverty line. De Certeau in *The Practice of Everyday Life* (1984) speaks cogently of the practices of the dominant culture in relation to the tactics and schemas of action manifest in what he terms the marginal, silent majority (36–8). His text is not concerned with dress, but if we

extend his ideas on social practices to clothing more generally, it can be
seen as an area in which social struggles are articulated in subtle and
sometimes more overt ways. So whilst dominant institutional culture may
be the official organ for design and production of clothes, non-privileged
groups can make use of clothing in inventive ways that signal their social
and political affiliations. Yet the notion of a dialectical struggle between
dominant and subordinate reinstates a series of binaries, and is thus
sometimes unhelpful to a study which seeks to explain why dress is chosen
and worn in ways that can be less categoric. Take for instance the Zambian
practice of *salaula*, or the picking out of select items of secondhand clothing
in street markets (Hansen 1994, 1999, 2000). In Zambia underprivileged
consumers are not exactly engaged in dialectical struggles for identity, since
they acquire goods just as affluent customers do elsewhere; it is simply
that their purchasing of cheap, sold-on goods from Europe is conducted
in a different framework from that of the west.

Although clothing still carries the 'baggage' of masculinity and femininity, particularly evident in the underdeveloped world, the conventional
binaries of 'male' and 'female', in the first world at least, seem to have
become less absolute than previously, particularly in leisure and sportswear.
With less absolute notions of gender come new spatial codes of wearing
that impact on dress. In the nineteenth century class and gender were
clearly denoted, especially in the dress of the middle classes, and particularly
in relation to occupation and social rituals. So the extent of habitable
territory for this class was largely determined by clothing. If a member of
a class moved out of his or her normal arena, their clothing tended to
betray incompatibility with location. Today this kind of prescriptive notion
of dress and spatiality, including social behaviour as indicative of core
status, has been transformed by a host of factors, including the tactical
adoption of clothing for effect, and the assumption of provisional identity.
It is further ameliorated by the virtual nature of many of our interactions.
In the words of Everard, 'we live in a world of surfaces that produce
identities at the intersection points between one surface and another'
(Everard 1999: 41). This is posited as a way of understanding the material
and symbolic culture of our social life as expressed in dress; the notion
of not only the networked society, but also the 'networked identity'.

Clearly a widening and global dissemination of knowledge and commerce in the postmodern age, based on the 'soft architecture' of the network,
increasingly defines our institutions, our practices and our subjectivities
(Peters and Roberts 1999: 52). Lefebvre in his text *The Production of Space*
(1991) argues that nowadays social space has an active instrumental role,
as it is constituted both by knowledge and action. This notion of space
is so diverse that commodities can neither be regarded as entity nor as

product. Things produced are subsumed, and their interrelationships encompassed, both in terms of their relative order and/or disorder (Lefebvre 1991: 73). Lefebvre claims 'Space "is" whole and broken, global and fractured at one and the same time. Just as it is at once conceived, perceived and directly lived' (Lefebvre 1991: 356). The basis of the whole, he suggests, is disassociation and separation, maintained as such by the will of the State from above, but pressure from below can confront the State and create what amounts to a counter-space. This schizoid space of both homogenisation and fragmentation has important implications for dress. Capitalism, which demands shorter time lapses between investment and return, is spatially compressing the world, whilst appearing simultaneously to enlarge the western world (Wassmann 1998: 8). But migrations from the periphery, and the periphery itself, militate against the stability of consensual compression. Globalisation therefore operates simultaneously at two levels, the overarching and the local. This is not entirely a case of mutual entanglement between cultures. Rather it is a series of unequal systems, homogenous and localised, between which various forms of tactical engagement can occur. More than this, even at the level of western homogenisation or cosmopolitanism, as Schoss suggests, there is not one, but a multiplicity of cosmopolitanisms (Schoss 1996: 184).

There is the further issue of time within the global. This relates to the compressed speed of information flows that create both virtual time and differential time in the same global space. A good example of this compression of time and tradition can be seen in an image of Her Majesty Queen Elizabeth receiving the credentials of the High Commissioner of the Republic of Zambia, S. K. Mubukwanu, of the royal house of Bulozi in 2001, disseminated world wide by the international press (Figure 5). The Queen's formal dress and almost ritualised hairdressing, is a lasting tribute to British style of the 1950s. By contrast the clothing of the High Commissioner occupies time periods whose differentials have been collapsed into a mixture of customary dress, a modern adaptation of past ceremonial dress and lastly current western dress. He is wearing a modernised modification of formal dress, traditionally worn for the *Kuomboka* ceremony in Western Zambia. This includes a version of the customary pleated skirt-like *siziba*, the cloth chosen for this occasion by his wife, and also an interpretation of the traditional red *lishushu* cap. About his shoulders is a *malesu* cloth (called elsewhere in Africa a *kanga* cloth).[4] His white shirt is an everyday business shirt and his shoes, rather than the more usual bare feet, came from a London shoe store.[5]

5 Queen Elizabeth, in a formal dress, meets the High Commissioner of Zambia in 2001. He wears a mixture of customary dress, modern modifications of dress traditionally worn for the *Kuomboka* Ceremony, and western garments

Modernity versus the customary

The image of the Zambian ambassador in official dress signals some of the complicating ways modernity and tradition are tangled together, as cultures negotiate their place in the global world. With the break up of colonial rule and struggles for national liberation and self-determination, clothing has inevitably been caught up in the ensuing tensions. Dress has frequently played a symbolic role, as revolutionary and/or new nationalist governments endeavour to establish themselves. Whilst the tensions that result from struggles between European style and local indigenous dress can be part of a nationalist agenda, it is not always so. European or American style dress, that stands for industrial progress, modernity and the west's cultural dominance, has gone through uneven developmental stages and degrees of acceptance and resistance. Initially perhaps it was imposed, or encouraged in new nations, and then either rejected or partially accepted. And whose version of a culture is authentic, the customary one practised by local people or a modified westernised version which is sometimes preferred by them? (Howes 1996: 187).

In non-western cultures, acceptance, rejection or a combination of western and traditional clothing is highly variable, complex and constantly changing. In West Africa, for instance, what is an intense fashion lexicon revolves around a dichotomous choice between traditional African and 'foreign' European dress (Mustafa 1998: 31). But there is also a case to be made for a pan African dress, a version of the *chitenge* dress for women that signifies a modern and not a traditional Africa (Hansen 2000: 264). In Nigeria, a sporadic acceptance of western dress has occurred, where tactical compromises between specific and local versions of western clothing and Nigerian dress have taken place over a number of generations. For instance, in the late 1980s, certain deliberate modifications were made to the customary voluminous male *agbada* tunic in Nigeria by lengthening it, and using dark not bright brocades, the colour copied from western dress. This was a deliberate tribute to tradition but couched in the language of the modern (Bastian 1996: 117–19). A different example can be shown in Senegal where western style suits worn by the political elite in President Sengor's rule (1960–80) were replaced more recently, under President Abdou Diouf, by Islamic style *boubous* and trousers (Mustafa 1998: 35), as a reinstatement of customary traditions. Africans who live in the UK have a different attitude about dress again, one that reflects their social circumstances. Immigrant Ghanaians in London, who do not yet consider themselves as fully British, continue to identify with their country of origin until they do. They buy goods in West African shops and send home gifts such as traditional West African cloth, in preference to what might have been regarded as exotic English items (Miller, D. 1998: 164–5).

In the process of modernisation or its rejection, women generally remain closer to traditional clothing than men, as we see in this image of a Somali family living in the suburb of Southall, in London. Here, customary dress is retained by the woman and not by her husband or her child (Figure 6). This retention of ethnic attire by women, as guardians of traditional culture is not unusual. A comparable situation is found in Indonesia. The indigenous *sarung* or *kain* and *kebaya* (wrap around skirt and blouse), reintroduced by elite women after Independence, is used mostly on public occasions and as a form of national costume for women (Nordholdt 1997: 13). This attire marks a strong contrast to that of Indonesian men. Their official formal attire can consist of either the safari suit, the long-sleeved batik shirt worn loose over trousers or the western suit. Protocol insists that only the long-sleeved batik shirt can be worn for official dinners (van Dijk 1997: 72). So quite clearly the 'traditional' dress of a culture is not necessarily fixed or static. It can undergo changes similar

6 A Somali family resident in Southall, London, 2001

7 These two young men, near a village well in Mauritania in 2003, wear customary dress, the man on the right wears his voluminous *boubou* over a western style shirt

to fashion, take various forms, have regional or imported inflections and be worn variously, dependent on the occasion. Friedman's notion of the systematic double articulation of the global being not chaotic, but a simultaneous standardisation and also fragmentation of local strategising, or even a balkanisation, seems a reasonable way to view such uneven dress practices.

From this it is clear that diasporic cultures or members of new nations do not adopt western dress without consideration. They draw selectively, and unevenly, on the clothes of dual cultural systems and for a variety of reasons. The overlay of a customary *boubou* onto a western style collared shirt by the young Mauritanian village man (Figure 7) shows clearly this dual usage. Fandy, in his important essay on the politics of Egyptian dress, demonstrates the complicated relationship between modern and traditional clothing in the power-laden context of big urban centres like Alexandria and Cairo. Here people weave in and out of western, Saudi style clothing and ethnic dress. Their choice depends on what they want to achieve, who they want to impress, who employs them, and on their religious beliefs.

Style is embodied in dress as well as in how you wear and manage your clothing. Throughout Egypt there are also geographical differences reflected in dress. Rural men in the north wear a form of *jallabia* different from those of the south who wear full bottomed *jallabias* practically all the time, unless they are working for the government which insists on European style dress. Northerners wear a wool *taqiya* or fez-like hat, whilst southerners wear a turban (Fandy 1998: 14)

As well as complicated uses of various types of region specific, customary and modern dress, cultures often revive or reinvent their past traditional clothing as they seek to reclaim past cultural practices. This acceptance of relativity in clothing practices is significant. Lefebvre's views on the instrumental role of social space are pertinent here, for social space, as demarcated by dress, can be encompassed by both modern mass uniformity, as well as the supposedly timeless and traditional, even the fragmented strategies of local style inflections. An interesting example to consider is the current revival of traditional dress in Asia. Younger Japanese people have been inclined to regard the traditional kimono as uncomfortable, although recently the unlined and cheaper summer version, the *yukata*, with unusual fabrics and non-traditional patterns, has been popularly revived. On the whole, modern Japanese people prefer to wear western clothing or *yofuku*. Even so, women are particularly encouraged to wear traditional Japanese attire, called *wafuku*, chiefly on ceremonial occasions such as coming-of-age celebrations. Importantly these ceremonial kimonos mark a shift from the numerous varieties of pre-modern kimono to a new, single-mode traditional style, and are thus a deliberate attempt to invent an occasion specific form of dress. Indeed, women who wear it demonstrate a form of femininity symbolic of tradition, but occurring in modern Japan (Goldstein-Gidoni 1999: 16).

As cultures evolve and develop, so too do the message requirements of their dress, and the relationship they have with western clothes and social practices. What happens when people move away from their country of origin adds further complications. When westerners visit places like Saharan Africa, India or Nepal there is often a desire to adopt local customary dress like headscarves, turbans, blouses or nose studs. Yet for those who leave the underdeveloped world, many demonstrate an increased desire to express their customary indigeneity in dress. But sometimes the reverse can happen, that is a desire to shed former practices and conform to the new environment. So, for migrants to the west there can be tension between practical attempts to assimilate with customs in the new country, and strength of loyalty to older dress practices. The latter can be affected by the season or event and by the age of the wearer. At the Hindu-Jain Temple in Murraysville, USA, Indian girls are westernised most of the time, only wearing Indian style clothing at very special events such as the sacred thread ceremony. Adult women are different for they wear more modest attire, such as a sari or *'punjabi'* outfit. This can be compared to the more conservative dress at the South Indian temple near Pittsburgh where young women more often wear Indian body attire like *punjabis* and *hindis* (B. D. Miller 1998: 272). All these examples show subtle relationships between past practices and modern accommodations are played out on a day-to-day basis in many diasporic cultures, and indeed as part of cultures that interweave with that of their hosts on a temporary basis.

In a global environment, it is often difficult to identify where a garment originates. The appearance of dress can seem remarkably uniform, and although local countries have their own industries, the complex production and marketing chain is unquestionably global. But we need to acknowledge a tension between the hegemony of western dress and the particular and personal aspects of local responses, some of which may involve retention of versions of traditional dress or even their reinvention. It is the present proposition that this relationship is not simply the case of a dominant style versus different versions or sets of marginal styles, resistant or otherwise. Even hybrid dressing is complicated and never absolute. Along-side customary dress there may be a qualified mixture of features that can include a substantial dissymmetry between the dominance of dress stemming from the US and Europe and elements derived from other cultures, ethnicities and minority groups. So it is often a question of unbalanced ways in which the universal and the particular function in relation to one another, or indeed as the multiplicity of cosmopolitanisms relate to localisms of all kinds.

Within the overarching uniformity of much global attire, patterns of wearing continue to exist that are locally distinctive. Wherever we choose to look, people are making quite particular, strategic and personally meaningful decisions about what to wear. It becomes virtually impossible to formulate a straightforward understanding of global identity and 'difference'. Fortunately there are certain recurring principles that can aid our comprehension. One of these is that globalisation is pervasive, even where there is the greatest resistance. Another is that people everywhere seek to demonstrate their identity, and cherish their difference. One might suggest a similar situation applies in the globalisation of food, sport and even technology. Yet any attempt to fully comprehend the capacity of global processes through analysis of dress requires an understanding of the range of theoretical positions that apply to the phenomenon of globalisation. Theories such as those espoused by Friedman, Craik, Lefebvre and others suggest global processes are neither uniform nor culturally chaotic. They are made up of different systems and 'flows', constituted both by sameness and various forms of strategic 'difference', that Friedman calls the double yet unbalanced articulation between the overarching and the local. Such theories can help us gain a clearer picture of what must be termed the fractured nature of global attire.

Notes

1 Friedman defines as fourth world those re-establishing cultural/political autonomy for indigenous peoples, such as Amerindians and Hawaiians (1994: 78).

2 www.worldbank.org/poverty/data/trends/income.htm, accessed September 2001.

3 See new work by Jane Bridgeman suggesting that sumptuary laws in Italy could be regarded as providing authorities with a wealth tax, derived from those who failed to adhere to their strictures. 'Pagare le pompe' (2000).

4 *Kanga* cloth is produced in Kenya but also in China, India and Arab countries. It is called *leso* in coastal areas of Kenya (Schoss 1996: 168).

5 I am most grateful to His Excellency Mr Mubukwanu for his willingness to share information about this occasion with me during an interview in London, December 2001.

2 ✧ Dress and global 'sameness'

The Sovs are becoming reasonably western looking, about like the
Munsters, but they still lag in necktie technology and wear
dirt-and-lint-coloured polyester stripes the width of a bedspread.
(P. J. O'Rourke 1988)

I N ORDER TO UNDERSTAND some of the processes at work in global
dress, we need to examine what appears on the surface to be an
overarching uniformity of clothing. Consumers of both sexes, from
Mexico City to London, New York, Moscow, Beijing and Sydney, increasingly seem to be dressing in low-key, often relatively gender neutral, western
style clothing. Even if we move further afield, well beyond the major cities

8 Men and women shopping in the mall, Winchester, 2001

9 Two Nepali boys wearing western clothing in the central square, Patan, Kathmandu in 1996. In the far background, a woman can be seen in customary clothing

of the developed world, to less urbanised and even rural areas, we can still find much the same kind of generic clothing being worn. With the exception of certain Muslim dominated countries, women dress in jeans, shorts or trousers, skirts, sometimes with jackets, jumpers, pumps or flat shoes, coats and blouses or T-shirts, whilst men wear a fairly standard range of garments that include business suits, T-shirts, buttoned shirts, windcheaters or anoraks and sweaters, short or long trousers, vests, trainers, beanies, sneakers and baseball caps. Obviously price and quality differ but everyday wear, including branded goods, are universally available and the garments appear to contain few distinguishing features. Young men in jeans, shirts, leisure jackets and sneakers, photographed in the central square of Patan, Kathmandu appear practically indistinguishable from youths shopping in the centre of Winchester, UK (Figures 8 and 9).

In one way it is possible to argue that this 'sameness' of dress, something Craik refers to as 'everyday fashion' (Craik 1994: 205), is the essence of global attire. In fact most people seem to think that the term global dress is synonymous with generic or homogenous clothing. Generic western style dress is a direct product of capitalism, and a global industrial capacity to produce and market mass volume clothes cheaply and easily. Feeding and augmenting this production is the pervasive influence of US culture and the force of branded goods promoted through television, film, advertising, and from the later 1990s, e-marketing. As Klein says, market driven globalisation does not want diversity; quite the opposite (Klein 2000: 129). This apparent consumption of fewer and fewer styles is undoubtedly linked to the sophisticated worldwide market penetration of the flagrantly branded multinational corporations. Eminently suited to the borderless domains of global commerce, these huge companies push sales of fairly uniform goods. They encourage the consumption of clothes in which the distinguishing feature is often merely the company logo or a certain colour scheme. The successful global company Jockey International, with headquarters in Wisconsin, markets its branded products in over 100 countries, with some 1,000 registrations of its trademarks and patents in 135 countries (Dickerson 1999: 445). So effectively has Jockey become part of the global language, that the brand name 'Jocks' as a term has replaced other words for underwear.

Incontrovertibly the advertising rhetoric of transnational companies such as Benetton, Gap, Diesel and Nike etc., and their successful promotion of a purportedly 'worldwide style culture', has significantly encouraged perceptions about global 'sameness' in dress. The fictional space and global advertising claims of Nike World, Diesel Planet and Benetton's One World, certainly at the end of the 1990s, deliberately created a soothing impression of universal order and harmony in clothing as in other areas of existence, denying cultural, political and racial differences, as well as national peculiarities (Gilbert 2000: 7). In this way the multinationals were able to convince consumers of their unsurpassed ability to deliver their products to a supposedly 'single, borderless macro culture' (Polhemus 1998: 20). This is a culture instantly accessible on hundreds of TV channels all around the world (LaFeber 1999: 56).[1] The driving concept of Diesel, the North Italian based casual clothing company, has been 'not "us" and "them", but simply one giant "we"', catering to a supposedly nationless, raceless world of consumers, where all their goods lack cultural specificity (Polhemus 1998: 54). Yet, at the same time, this kind of rhetoric is countermanded by claims that the individual customer and their preferences matter to the global giants. Whilst there are signs that consumer fight back and subversive brand 'adbusting' has begun in earnest, the degree of success achieved by protestors against the colossal power of these branded companies has been limited.[2] One reason is that all publicity is good publicity and they have simply transformed adverse criticism about themselves into further profitable advertising (Bell 2001: 95).

A key factor in successful worldwide marketing practices is the power and effect of the logo. This topic has recently been the subject of a number of critical assessments, including the very successful book by Naomi Klein

No Logo (2000). Authors like Evans, Lury and Klein have shown, amongst other things, that globalisation of dress is synonymous with the youth market. Nike's 'Swoosh' symbol and Air Jordan shoes encapsulate the 'air' or free flying spatiality, so sought after by extreme sports-mad youth, while baggy jeans, oversized basketball shoes, baseball cap worn backwards and hooded sweatshirt, have become the archetypal global costume of the skateboarder. Nike and Reebok have actually built their empires on the tastes of young people, the irony being that company 'cool hunters' appropriate the designs of poor blacks and Latino youths, and immediately sell their own style back to them at hugely inflated prices. As Klein says, the fundamental irony of these global giants is that the people most hurt in terms of high prices are blacks, who infused their logos with meaning and from whom they have taken most (Klein 2000: 369). So the promotion of logos now operates in a global fashion economy where the commodity has transmogrified beyond actual clothing, into an unchecked circulation of signs, meanings and network of relations. These relate to more than the 'genuine' logo garment, which is only part of the picture, for many look-alike clothes are patently brand fakes, adding another dimension to the nature of brands. Logos are not goods. They are fundamentally desirable images and concepts. As such they permeate everywhere. Freed from co-ordinates of time, place and economic status, these markers remind us that nothing in our world can escape being commodified (Giroux 1993–94: 13).

There is more irony in the fact that while clothing companies like Nike operate in terms of enfolding all within their universal brand consciousness, many global clothing corporations purport at the same time to be demand-driven. One such company is Benetton, the huge transnational Treviso company, probably the first middle-market fashion chain to go global, which had 7040 shops all over the world by 1992 (Crewe and Lowe 1996: 275).[3] Constituted by a number of sportswear labels like Playlife and Killer Loop, and sports equipment, as well as the major brands of United Colors of Benetton and Sisley, the company is dedicated to immediately spotting preferences and differentials of purchasers (Giroux 1993–94: 17). Their highly mechanised production plant near Treviso has a built-in interactive and rapid response to customer tastes, as well as directly controlled 'foreign production poles' and subcontracting networks (Camuffo *et al.* 2001: 47–9). Stock levels are automated, trends can be spotted immediately and exploited, and stores worldwide can be assigned stock in seven days (49). This is very different from the practice of predicting styles or imposing them, previously more usual in the fashion industry. So, within the landscape of worldwide product distribution and their novel concept of vertical integration management, Benetton's corporate ideology maintains a high degree of flexibility that supposedly reflects specific market trends and the particularity of taste in diverse groups (Camuffo *et al.* 2001: 47). At the same time, it promotes a simultaneous unification of such 'differences', within their concept of a 'world without borders' (Giroux 1993–94: 18). This demonstrates Benetton's canny understanding both of the nature of globalisation and the current segmentation of the market.

Benetton purports to be fully responsive to consumer needs and able to provide them with the notion if not the actuality that they can access a dreamland of endless product choices, local preferences and possibilities. But what exactly is this supposed 'difference' in branded dress that purports to service the individual tastes of consumers? Are branded clothes different or universally similar? Highly successful companies like Reebok and Nike, who produce the most powerful images, seem to be everywhere. Yet they own the least plant, obscure the circumstances in which their clothing is made and ostensibly employ the fewest workers (Klein 2000: 4). One must ask if such massive profit, based on highly skilled marketing, can incorporate genuine differentiation? Klein claims this is not the case. She exposes the undifferentiated manufacturing practices of numbers of big name brands in free-trade zones of third world towns, for instance Rosario, South of Manila. She says, 'Here competing labels aren't segregated each in its own superstore; they are often produced side by side in the same factories, glued by the very same workers, stitched and soldered on the very same machines' (Klein 2000: 203). Actual goods like trainers, caps and shirts can all look pretty much the same, whilst a plethora of types, models and branded logos have sprung up, with more released each year. It seems these are in effect simply the marketing of 'difference', actually papering over genuine factors of similarity.

Complicating factors

It is important, in any study of global clothing, to consider ways in which the marketing of the worldwide brand or logo fits with actual dress practices, and whether this is quite the same as homogenisation. In other words we need to examine what is meant by global 'sameness' with a degree of critical attention. One of the complicating factors is that people still exert personal choice about what they wear. This may include suits and jeans, both universal style garments, but these are often selected and worn with quite particular aims in mind. So whilst no one would deny that there is a tendency for people worldwide to look similar to most others, even in branded gear, and that convergence of style is a major aspect of global dressing, this is complicated by many factors such as market segmentation and personal preferences. Ostensibly the students in this photograph (Figure 10) look similarly dressed, even lacking much in the way of gender or

10 Students of both sexes but different racial backgrounds in Brisbane, Australia 2002. They all wear unspecific and quite similar looking mass produced trousers, sporting or leisure shoes and long sleeved shirts

racial differentiation. Yet their clothing may be subject to micro details understandable primarily to their particular social subgroup. There is also a quite evident middle-market liking for understatement in dress that fails to identify, as exemplified by the moderately priced, unexceptional Japanese Uniqlo label launched in 2001. This is an almost anonymous style, quiet, universal and functional, focusing on wearability and lack of design dogmatism that is itself a particular version of 'sameness'.

So is there such a thing as a typical or generic male suit, pair of jeans or baseball cap, or is it the case that such clothes seem uniform only to the uninformed? Are we perhaps assuming that everyone is succumbing to universal branding or uninteresting and undifferentiated US-style clothing, thus failing to see the intricacies of global dress? Perhaps it is primarily company rhetoric and immensely perspicacious marketing that has led to this belief. Some authors argue that the 1990s witnessed the decline not only of the mass market but also of the middle market, and that there remain simply market segments (Humphrey 1998: 156). If this is the case, can we reconcile a fully segmented market with a supposed universalised form of clothing? Looking at the statistics of clothing production around the world, the US was the sixth largest clothing exporter in 1994 (Productivity Commission 1997: 251). And in 1996 the US became the world's leading importer rather than exporter of apparel, to the amount of US$43.32 billion, with Germany second at $24.10 billion (Dickerson 1999: 105). Much of this clothing comes from China, who was leading the world in textile and apparel supply by the early 1990s (Productivity Commission 1997: 119). In 1998 China had a garment output of 9.7 billion clothing items, although at that time still had practically no brand names registered in the international market (Yunfeng 1999: 1). To regard the US as a dominating player in the production of dress is difficult to reconcile with such statistics.

Evidentially there has been a marked shift in the composition of the top apparel exporters of the world away from nations like the US, to countries like China. But in a global marketplace we cannot assume stable or homogeneous consumption patterns. The percentage of household consumption of footwear and clothing is much higher for example in Tanzania than in Switzerland (Dickerson 1999: 181). Equally significant is an understanding of the operational nature of the textile and apparel industries around the world. Not long ago, these industries were made up of nationally independent sectors and markets. In the modern world anything can be made anywhere and sold anywhere. While the rhetoric of a British or Australian fashion industry may currently be promoted, it is almost impossible to describe clothing as being characteristic of say, Africa, South America or Indonesia. The Mexicans still regard Nike products made in Mexico as American clothes (Howes 1996: 194). Determining the precise origin of garments which may be designed in one country, assembled in another and worn somewhere else is a convoluted exercise. A product may be created in many different countries and be re-exported, as Hong Kong does with products from China (Dickerson 1999: 210), whilst fashion conscious Hong Kong consumers look to Japan for the latest style, for more appropriate sizes and quality, not the US. Countries like the US send cut garment pieces to Mexico and the Caribbean for assembly. The finished garments are then returned to the US for marketing and distribution (Dickerson 1999: 230).[4] So products may be made in one context, marketed in another and the choice and consumption of articles likely to be inflected by factors of age, gender local tastes and preferences all making the notion of universal 'sameness' difficult to sustain.

Another factor that mitigates against uniformity is that many high street chains and global online companies, GAP and Lands' End Store to name two, produce higher grades of basic, homogenous clothing than others. Private labels too are a feature of upscale retailers such as Barney's, Bendel's and Bergdorf (Blau 1999: 141). Such superior class labels are produced with the capacity for considerable mark-up and with increased direct retail input into design, yet still have generic elements (Lowe and Wrigley 1996: 11). Paradoxically even generic attire is now being marketed back to consumers, as a form of minimalist fashion.[5] Indeed there are a number of levels of global 'sameness' that operate at any one time. So we find complicated tensions between dominant styles (sold through mass merchandisers and supermarkets), specialist lines produced by chains like Next, and more localised manufacturing activities and products. The latter insinuate themselves in the cracks between corporate and mainstream marketing practices, and selling-on practices characteristic of the grassroots economy. All of these constitute what Gilbert terms 'local taste constella-tions', that to a greater or lesser degree mitigate against notions of universality (Gilbert 2000: 12).

The deliberate 'casualisation' of dress in the workplace, so called 'dress-down Fridays', which itself has some components of uniformity and 'sameness' further complicates issues of supposed global uniformity. Ad-vertising, media and dot. com executives lead the way with this relatively casual dress that seems set to continue for the foreseeable future. Even conservative Wall Street firms began to accept more informal clothes during the late 1990s, at least for part of the working week. In 2001 a poll, conducted among American companies by the Society for Human Resource Management, claimed 86 per cent of US companies allowed some form of casual dress (Munoz 2001: 1). But even to link casual wear with globalised clothing is not without contradictions. Some garments, like generic style tracksuits and runners, were originally conceived as quite unspecific forms of leisurewear. They have now been co-opted as fashion-able items, carry branded logos, and can be made in seasonal colours or are linked to 'lifestyle' products. So the degree to which this clothing is genuinely global is a matter of interpretation.

If we look at the other side of the spectrum, at the consumption of clothing at the level of the very lowest socio-economic groups, the degree to which generic secondhand clothing is worn worldwide is astonishing. Much of this clothing originates from the US and Europe, supposedly further extending notions of homogeneity. For instance large companies like FOB Miami, North American Trade Associates Inc and Martin Rood of Amsterdam, export huge quantities of baled secondhand clothes and footwear to underdeveloped countries, especially Africa and India. They sell unsorted mixtures of these bales, of fairly homogenous clothes (at a minimum of 100 lbs weight), or alternatively bales sorted into categories like shirts, trousers, jeans and so on at a slightly higher price. These are imported into countries like Zambia and Ghana where the practice of on-selling is extremely widespread.

Alternatively the poor in Africa and India wear cast-off dress. A group of Malian Bambara children photographed in the village of Worontona Falena in 1996, far from the coast, are evidently wearing charity or secondhand clothing, as the labels on their garments and accessories would indicate (Figure 28). A Swiss Academy for Development study of the impact of donated secondhand clothing on underdeveloped countries published on the internet in 1998, found 95 per cent of Ghanaians surveyed wore cast off clothing.[6] Hansen claims used clothing was the eighth largest US export to sub-Saharan Africa in 1994. She quotes figures at that time that estimate one-third of sub-Saharan Africans were wearing charity or low cost European and American clothing, clearly of a fairly general type (Hansen 1994: 508). But what is most interesting is that African consumers are not undiscerning. They pick and choose from goods on offer in markets and stalls, and alter them as well, in ways that match their own personal style and local sartorial conventions. Consumers select not only preferred items, but in some cases choose imported secondhand goods over local secondhand clothes. The reason being not only price but they also seem to be 'new' and 'fresher' (Hansen 1999: 16).[7] All of this complicates any notion of a universalising of dress, and supports theories of the fractured nature of global clothing processes.

If the middle income consumer wears generic style clothing by choice, low income earners in the developed and the underdeveloped world, may have little or no flexibility. So the uptake of western dress, and indeed its different types of garment, varies according to preference, locale or region, to gender, to occasion, ethnicity and even to level of caste. With increased ethnic diversity in the US, for instance, market segmentation has engendered different tastes and buying habits. At the end of the twentieth century, Asian Americans and Hispanic Americans were identified as the fastest growing minorities in the US. Kang and Kim found the degree of acculturation of such immigrants affected their consumer choice (Kang and Kim 1998: 27). So even diverse levels within a single ethnic group can affect purchases and preferences for particular brands. All of this supports Friedman's assertions about a complicated and simultaneous relationship between global homogeneity and a sense of local variations and particularities.

There is little doubt that subtle and differentiated meanings and senses of identity circulate around western dress, despite its superficial uniformity. For this reason it is extremely problematic to speak categorically of a garment being generic within a global framework, although many garments do fall within this overarching term. Aside from this, cultural and economic reasons may make it imperative in many countries to continue wearing customary dress, at least on some occasions. So western style should not be regarded as entirely hegemonic. In one way it is possible to suggest that western clothing industries, even with factories unlikely to be located there, do mass produce garments that look remarkably similar. But these garments are not necessarily worn in similar ways, as any walk down any high street will show. Dress in the global arena is patently the physical marker of the tension or struggle between consensus, individual preferences and economic circumstances. Clearly, it is in the very act of making a choice that individuals assert their own tastes and proclivities.

Hierarchy and difference

Generic clothing is quite complicated in terms of its relationship to value added elements of 'difference' and novelty that is termed 'fashion'. While the focus of this chapter is on the supposed universality of dress and its meanings, one question we need to address is whether or not status and hierarchy can be communicated by wearing generic or relatively uniform clothing. Is such clothing truly egalitarian? The answer to this must be an emphatic no. Global clothing may appear to be largely undifferentiated, but its wearing certainly is not. Aside from ethnic preferences, differences exist between urban and rural dwellers, between young and old and also clearly between the economically middle of the road and the wealthier consumer, the latter of course able to purchase more up market clothing. Within alleged 'sameness' of style, there are clear variations of fabric quality, stitching, and to an extent of pattern. Moreover it is precisely the monetary freedom to choose amongst a variety of garments that marks out such differences. As Crane points out, by the late twentieth century there were considerable intricacies of relationships both between social groups and income levels that belie any illusion of integration. Democratisation of clothing has in fact led to diversity and not standardisation (Crane 2000: 240).

What makes consumption elite, though, has changed considerably since the early twentieth century, when considerable focus was placed on visible fashionability. Whilst echoes of sharply hierarchical differences of class as endorsed by fashion remain, there is no one elite class but clearly a pluralism of groups. As Herbert Blau succinctly notes, unprecedented diversity of attire has been diffused 'in a labyrinth of circulation, far more so than can be accounted for by distinctions of class' (Blau 1999: 135). Evidence can be found in the fact that the moneyed classes still demonstrate their power and influence through fashion and appearance, but the nature of their display has become more diffuse. Wealth and position are more likely to be indicated by accessories, such as shoes, bags and watches, by the stylishness of owning the latest technology, by grooming, by the level of fitness, travel opportunities, membership of a gym, real estate, or even by owning intangible luxuries such as perfumes, rather than simply clothing alone. Having said this, highly exclusive couture exists increasingly in uneasy relationship to its flagship diffusion lines that act as a kind of loss leader to enhance its prestige (Moore *et al.* 2000: 13)

One of the most interesting paradoxes within global marketing is the issue of customisation and DIY style. This can be usefully explored by examining the creation of the 'special' customer by on-line shopping sites. These sites mark a nexus between taste imposed on the consumer and the acknowledgement that, for those who can afford access to technology, taste can be individualistic, fragmented and personal. So internet retailing offers a certain personalisation of goods and customer feedback on a hitherto unimagined scale. In a sense e-shoppers are led to believe they dictate style rather than the other way around. Sites like www.landsend.com (the site of the Lands' End Store that commenced in 1995) make recommend- ations almost incestuously to their targeted consumers, based on a range of data collected from them.[8] This may include previous purchases, offline shopping, merges with other data gatherers or personal information freely given to the company (Berry 2000: 50). www.landsend.com has particular customised links such as 'Your Personal Model', where you can build your own virtual body and get advice on appropriate clothing, and 'Oxford Express', where you can sort through fabrics and styles. Some news filled sites, www.bolt.com for example, encourage consumers to spot trends, and this information feeds back into company data about momentary styles on the street. The reward to companies, and allegedly to consumers, is that the information gathered can be used to pinpoint the 'special' pur- chasers' desired goods and services. Technology is acting as a form of filter, actually supporting the creation of consumer hierarchies.

It is the proposition of this book that clothing remains as deeply meaningful to a global world as it did two centuries ago, even though high fashion is less obviously or widely worn. 'Sameness' of dress is what one may perceive if one looks at people from a certain distance going about their daily affairs. But a closer look reveals a complex minefield of information and market segmentation. So at the micro level of observation, and to someone well versed in the consumption practices of a culture, dress exudes small clues and meaningful details relating to features as minor as the colour of a tie, a type of earring or a shoe design. Even if the practice of high fashion in Europe and the US is somewhat more limited than fifty years ago, urban life continually reminds its occupants that they are subject to the scrutiny of others, a scrutiny that becomes a major factor in any choice of dress.

In a recent essay, Gilbert has examined the paradoxical relationship between the few large cities like Paris, New York and London, which claim to be prime and innovative sites of fashion, and the borderless even deregulated macro culture and geography integral to global marketing. The essay shows that whilst the facts of the 'flexible geography of production' become more and more invisible, cities as centres of consumption inevitably undergo radical transformation. Actual and conceptual links to fashion remain strong, if uneasy, even in these places (Gilbert 2000: 22). Making a city fashionable is part of creating a new symbolic economy for urban areas. This includes funding of museums and art galleries, elegant shopping venues, music, and gastronomy, all part of the culture industry. We continue to speak of a French, British or American fashion industry centred on a country's major metropolitan areas. But set against the sense of modern urban life as vibrant, intense and fashionably creative, is the fact that the majority of city dwellers, themselves global consumers, are unable to afford high fashion of any kind. They are low-key consumers of mass produced goods of uncertain origin. Interestingly then the myth and mystique of fashion still remains, if not always its full-blown practice.

The suit

One of the major contributing factors to a sense of sameness in the modern world is the two-piece suit, worn by professional men and women almost everywhere. Colours range between brown, grey and black, with slight variations in lapel sizes and vents, usually worn with a long sleeved shirt and tie, or for women a blouse. The suit is surely a global uniform for the management classes. In fact the acquisition of western-style suits has been a homogenising factor in the world, a sign of the acceptance of western values: 'the Japanese business man, the Arab Minister, the Indian lawyer, the African civil servant have all found a common denominator in the western suit' (Mazrui 1970: 22). Interestingly China's younger generation of post Mao leaders deliberately replaced the former blue Mao jacket with suits and ties, at the thirty-fifth anniversary celebration of the People's Republic of China in 1984. By this time the Mao jacket had penetrated even into far Western China. This is evident in a photograph of Muslim Kyrgyz men bargaining at the sheep market in Kashgar, Xinjiang region in 1987, wearing these cheap padded jackets (Figure 11). The old man on the left wears a doppa hat, signifying he comes from Kashgar and is a member of the Uyghur minority in Xinjiang.[9] So while most Chinese were still wearing the Mao style jacket, politicians in Beijing started to reverse the trend. Their show of suits was an explicit affirmation of change, a new acceptance of western dress codes and with this change the desire to make political links with the west (Li 1998: 77).

The suit in its modern and classic form, according to Hollander, is a

11 Kyrgyz men wearing Mao jackets at Kashgar, Xinjiang region, western China in 1987

heady mix of abstract formality, superiority, seriousness and strong mas-culine sex appeal (Hollander 1995: 113–14). It lends upper management and professional credibility, occasions feelings of trust, and its very ubiquity functions powerfully as a kind of global corporate glue. Look at the media coverage of any international business meeting, trade conference or sitting of parliament and one will certainly be exposed to a panorama of western style tailored suits. This clothing bears the desirable imprint of the success of capitalism and of professional status. While there are many theories put forward to explain the continuity of suit wearing by professional people, with associated meanings of stability and power, the assessment of men's dress has been the subject of well deserved revision. Craik, for instance, challenges the mythology that men's dress, primarily the suit, is an unchanging uniform. She shows there are cycles of fashion in men's dress, as in women's dress, although they have been expressed differently. Many groups of men use clothes in a variety of ways to express their own forms of masculinity and tastes, some clearly against the mainstream (Craik 1994: 176–9). In fact the 1980s witnessed a culture change in the ways in which men dressed. The emergence of the so called 'new man', supposedly with a new found interest in appearance, showed evidence of important changes to the nature of male consumption, diminishing the deep gender divide evident in mainstream dressing.

What is most interesting is the global belief that the suit is the necessary garment for the conduct of business. This may be attributable initially to classic manuals like John Molloy's *Dress for Success* (1975). Molloy's preferred garment was the suit. In his manual he claimed to be able to help executives and their staff look successful (even minority groups) and most importantly he assured readers he could help them increase their sales (Molloy 1975: 147–8). Manuals of this kind had a tremendous influence on the dress practices of the corporate sector. Even so there was a downturn in suit sales in the 1990s (Crane 2000: 174). They were replaced by 'dress-down' clothes, so called 'American East Coast off duty', intended to foster a more co-operative workplace allowing far greater individuality. This did not entirely eventuate. In fact 'smart casual' really meant the introduction of a new kind of coded uniformity, with a combination of chinos, polo or button down shirts and deck shoes, all in conservative navy or beige (York 1999: 99). 'Smart casual', being closer to leisurewear, challenged the homogeneity of suits but was itself another sort of uniform. It simply functioned at a lower key. With the downturn of the dot. com market, the formal business suit made something of a comeback, with predictions that suits would be reinstated as a business dress code. But it is likely the suit will remain only one among many options open to the business world, which is ostensibly, but perhaps not actually, homogeneously dressed.

Molloy followed up his manual for men with a manual for women, *Women: Dress for Success* (1980). He was thus instrumental in helping to define a way of dressing for the business and executive woman of the 1980s, something which came to be known as 'power dressing' (Entwistle 1997: 311). Women were encouraged to wear tailored suits that would place them alongside men in suits. It was a form of attire, ostensibly concerned with female empowerment in the male dominated workplace; one that enabled them to walk the compromisingly thin line between conventional notions of 'femininity' and 'masculinity' (Entwistle 2000b: 229). This uniform-like, supposedly non-sexual, dress was intended to demonstrate women had careers in the corporate workplace, a way for them to self manage their appearances rather than have a clothing code imposed (Entwistle 1997: 319). Whatever the case, women's suits have contributed to that sense of corporate homogeneity in appearance that one encounters in all major urban centres of the world. The suit, both for men and women, is the archetypal dress of 'sameness' that acts to diminish gender difference and strengthen corporate allegiance. However one must regard its alleged uniformity with some scepticism.

Indeed, if we imagine the uniform-like suit is an index of modern progress and urbanisation, this is not strictly correct. Suits vary in quality, fabric, cut and price. Practices of wearing also differ considerably dependent on the wearer's organisational status (Crane 2000: 174). Suits signal subtly different meanings to different cultures, and indeed to western subgroups as well. Subcultural groups in Europe and the US have used suits in a number of ways, to parody the establishment, to signal the non-orthodox or as evidence of group identity. Dot. com executives might wear a suit, but with a bright shirt without a tie and dreadlocks; pop stars and actors often wear non-orthodox designs in unusual fabrics and colours, usually without ties, perhaps with Nehru style jackets. So the suit may be a solid symbol of respectability in business culture in Europe and the US, but beyond in many parts of the Middle East, India and Asia, suits, shirts and trousers certainly carry western meanings, but not all the time or in all manifestations. In fact they are sometimes combined with regional or religious accessories like the Jewish *yarmulke* cap. In Indonesia, conventional suits have quite specific meanings related to western progress but also to power and masculine authoritarianism, a vestige of the dress attitudes of past colonial rulers. On the other hand they do not signal civil participation in national politics. This is more the meaning associated with batik shirts (Nordholt 1997: 12).

In Egypt there are differences again. It is customary for men to wear business suits if they are working for the government, or in businesses associated with westerners. But after work they usually change back into their own indigenous dress, *jallabias*. In upper Egypt villagers wear full *jallabias* and a huge turban and carry a staff the height of a man. Importantly, in contrast to the west, this clothing rather than the suit is identified with masculine power. So, if a villager wears western dress, or is compelled for some reason to wear it, it may signify immaturity, even the unmanly compared to traditional dress (Fandy 1998: 5–6). What is also interesting is that in Cairo the Saudi style *jallabia*, not the southern or northern *jallabia*, actively competes with western business clothing as a similar sign of cosmopolitanism, wealth and power (Fandy 1998: 8). So the business suit is not a universal corporate symbol.

Jeans

One of the most significant garments that have given rise to the belief in global uniformity is jeans. Shabby or stylish, jeans are an all-purpose form of dress that can be worn by anyone, men and women, young and old, well off and poor throughout the world, in any country. Wearers include subcultural group members, street vendors, students, tradespeople, farmers, as well as the well-heeled urbanite. As Dant claims, jeans are hard wearing garments that all look more or less the same, pretty classless and non-gendered, thus having no inherent meaning in themselves. This makes them quite unlike the tailored suit which through its intrinsic 'look' imposes significant meaning (Dant 1999: 102 and 106–7). Herein lies the universal usefulness and significance of jeans.

Jeans are regarded as an archetypal product of America. If Indian women wear western dress rather than indigenous attire, they often prefer to wear jeans rather than skirts and dresses, regarding jeans as American, and thus without the residual meanings associated with colonial occupation (Tarlo 1996: 335). The question might be how stylistically undifferentiated are jeans, and to what extent are they 'American'? Originally practical working garments for men, they gained credibility from movie stars like Marlon Brando and James Dean who wore them, and they were endemic to the youth revolution of the 1960s. To a large degree they have remained significant ever since. Levi Strauss has been the most significant of all the companies marketing jeans, challenged more recently by Wrangler, Lee, Gap and others. Even secondhand Levi's are a large selling line for giant clothing firms like Evans Distributors, Canton, Ohio, who sell used jeans either by the pound, or by the pair if they are A grade.[10] Whatever the reason, it is certainly the marketing strength of a company like Levi Strauss, coupled with their cinematic connections, that has led to the perception that jeans can be readily associated with wholesome American values.

Yet the history of jeans shows they are neither uniform nor unvarying. In fact jeans are garments which, in Dant's terms, have no intrinsic meaning and thus are available for meaning to be imposed. Perhaps more importantly, jeans are signature garments, for wearers themselves clearly customise their own garments in all kinds of ways by the very fact of being used; jeans are variously worn, faded, torn, embroidered, patched and so on. Even their shape fits the body of their wearer in intimate ways. In addition, over the years there have been numerous fashion changes, including style revivals in jeans. Customisation has entered the jeans market too. In 2002 Just Jeans in Australia marketed fashionable jeans with thigh areas individually whitened with fabric guns, so that each pair looked different. The other point is that not all jeans are American-made. Any close analysis of a pair of jeans might show that their component parts come from an international range of sources. The cotton material might be grown in Africa, stone washed in Tunisia, dyed in Italy using synthetic indigo from Germany, stitched somewhere else, using zips from Japan and probably but not necessarily designed in New York (Abrams and Astill 2001: 1). This complication seems to make jeans the perfect postmodern garment. At the same time they are quite generally believed to be honest, neutral, egalitarian, almost gender unspecific and 'authentic'. What more could you ask of a global garment?

Western style clothing is certainly the dominating mode of dress today, universally accepted and worn. Yet it has been unevenly taken up across the world, for the migratory flows of clothing production and consumption within our global environment are far more complex than we might at first assume. Mathews has suggested that the precise relation between globally available products and the sense consumers have of their own cultural identity remains unclear (Mathews 2000: 18). Generic clothing goods, but also food, furniture, home décor and so on, available in what Mathews terms the 'cultural supermarket', override, but also contradict, the consumer's sense of a single national or ethnic identity. So using dress to signal one's identity or ethnicity remains crucial in the complexities of modern life. In fact, in the less developed world, generic western type clothing is often simply tactically assumed in order to partake of perceived benefits that accrue to such dressing. That is, it can be put on when the need arises, and just as easily removed. Herero women, for instance, prefer to wear customary dress at home but western dress for work (Durham 1999: 395). Over any short period an Indonesian man may wear a western style suit for business, tour the country in a so-called safari suit, wear a modern batik shirt for a reception and a regional costume for a wedding ceremony (van Dijk 1997: 40). This means that in some cultures western dress appears to have higher value for certain occasions than for others (Molnar 1998: 41).

Clearly it is possible to be Chinese, Japanese or South American by nationality and cultural background whilst at the same time, and to one degree or another, have access to the global supermarket of style. Advertisement of global goods is supported by media monopolies in the hands of TV channels originating in the US, Britain and, to an extent, France. Yet tensions are emerging with deregulation of the media and the rise of a multiplicity of information sources via the internet. Consumer choice is also inflected by many factors of taste, gender, ethnicity, level of income and sexuality. These can be quite subtle. For instance a Chinese woman wearing up-market Chinese clothes may not have the precise sense of style and comportment that allows her to avoid derogatory labelling by Hong Kong residents (Mathews 2000: 22). For years Hong Kong had the world-wide reputation of being a garment manufacturing centre that dealt in cheap versions and garment copies (Clark 2000: 83). Yet people in Hong Kong have become critics of the clothes of visitors from mainland China. So, while one acknowledges there is a 'sameness' of attire evident throughout the world, encouraged and promoted by worldwide media monopolies, it is a uniformity touched with countless subtle variations and differences. Sameness is conjoined with such a variety of elements and repertoires drawn from local cultures, that it could be described as a qualified uniformity, much the same as the uniformity we acknowledge in other cultural categories.

Notes

1 In 1991 Nike was the first to co-ordinate one of these round-the-world commercials to sell their New Air 180 shoe, priming viewers initially with entertaining Super Bowl game spots, featuring Michael Jordan and others (LaFeber 1999: 67).

2 Ballinger claims that protests against Nike did help to raise the minimum wage in Indonesia between 1988 and 1996, but that there is essentially little to show in terms of other improvements in manufacturing practices (Ballinger 2001: 34–5).

3 Benetton's 2002 website maintained they produced about 100 million casual and sports garments a year, but had reduced the number of outlets they had in the past. The company had a consolidated revenue in the first half of 2001 of 1,044 million euro, www.benetton.com, accessed November 2001 and February 2002. By the end of 2000 Benetton had opened more than 60 retail huge outlets (megastores), expected more in 2001, and hoped for 100 such stores worldwide by the end of 2002. Apart from clothing, in 2002 they were selling sports equipment, cameras, nappies, fragrances, bags, CDs and house paint.

4 The Uruguay Round Agreements passed by USA Congress in 1994 set out some general principles for determining the country of origin of all textile and clothing products, a significant factor in determining quotas of goods allowed into the US.

5 For instance in 2001, Target stores, with branches in Australia and the US, launched its Basics Collection, self-consciously marketing the very generic features of clothes that they had been selling for many years.

6 www.sad.ch/monitoring#/garment.html, accessed April 2001.

7 This is somewhat different from the Tanzanian description of this clothing as the dress of those who had died in Europe (Weiss 1996: 138).

8 Lands' End Store is quite clear that its customer base is college educated and that two-thirds of its customers are professional people, www.landsend.com, accessed July 2001.

9 My thanks to Louise Beynon, Department of Anthropology, School of Oriental and African Studies, London, for this information.

10 www.evansdist.net, accessed July 2001.

3 ✧ Political dress

The crowd was impressive both in size and in its discipline. 'Freedom volunteers' wearing black, green and yellow armbands met the delegates and arranged their seating. There were old women and young wearing Congress skirts, Congress blouses, Congress *doekies* (scarves) old men and young wearing Congress armbands and Congress hats. Signs everywhere said FREEDOM IN OUR LIFETIME. LONG LIVE THE STRUGGLE. Congress of the People near Johannesburg, 1955. (Mandela 1994)

SOUTH AFRICA's Nelson Rolihlahla Mandela was one of the major political figures of the twentieth century.[1] From the early 1990s he used the striking and colourful 'Madiba' shirt as his personal political signature. With no specific links to traditional African dress, this distinctive outfit nevertheless came to symbolise the Mandela form of benign national-ism. By contrast his former wife, the controversial Winnie Madikizela, frequently appeared on public occasions wearing abundant gold jewellery, turban-like hats and beaded hairstyles, all dramatising her more aggressive brand of politics.[2] Signature dress of this kind is not solely the preserve of high profile politicians. Clothing can also be read as a sign of the political throughout the social spectrum, including at a grassroots level. When angry anti WTO, WEF, IMF and multinational corporation protesters put black masks or bandanas over their faces, wear slogan T-shirts with buzz cuts or dreadlocks, and use heavy boots to participate in civil street protests, they demonstrate that anti-mainstream clothing is also located within the sphere of the political.

So in one way it is possible to argue that all clothing is routinely bound up with politics. As the Comaroffs show in their essay on African Zionist attire, 'bodily signification ... is an inevitable component of all social practice: neither the most ethereal of expressions nor the most pragmatic of politics can escape being acted out through the human frame' (Comaroff 1992: 89). The various models of politicised attire under discussion are best understood if we regard them as signs of the shifts, struggles and social dislocations in the changing configurations of power within globalisation. These shifts are manifest in the diversification of mainstream and radical politics, in redefinitions of citizenship, and in religious tensions. They are especially evident in resurgences of national cultures in the aftermath of colonialism. Political dress specifically speaks to a worldwide, media savvy, sometimes unidentified audience. Its meanings draw on changing relations between the real and the symbolic, inextricably part of the complicated spatial logic of our times.

In this chapter the specific purpose of examining the relationship between dress, globalisation and politics, at upper levels of political activity as well as grass roots politics, is twofold. The concern lies firstly with the material accoutrements and appearance of political leaders and their con-sorts, and the degree to which 'style' is now deemed fundamental to the political process itself. Style is however a fluctuating even perfidious concept, and for politicians one of the dangers lies in the difficulty of dressing to preserve trust, whilst still looking up-to-date and acceptably stylish. It is therefore important to examine how clothes are devised, even stage managed for media attention, and so used to further global political ends. The changing tactics of such dress can attract intense, sometimes excessive press interest, understood as much by leaders of newly developing countries as in the west. When state officials assume specifically nationalist garments, for instance, it can be a calculated way to signal solidarity with working people, and by implication to gather more votes, as with *hanbok* wearing by conservative women legislators in Korea (Soh 1992: 383).[3] But it may also be a way of showcasing and promoting national feelings of solidarity, marking changes in the wake of colonial rule.

The second concern is to examine ways in which dress is implicated in grassroots or direct action political resistance, in contradistinction to attire assumed by those involved in institutionalised politics. This reading of protest dress supports Szerszynski's analysis of the ritualised, performative nature of direct action environmental protests, and his argument that sensitivity to these events can make us more mindful of the performative nature of politics generally. In fact he suggests that mainstream political life is as performative as the non-mainstream, the two simply operate according to different cultural logics or 'dramaturgies of human action' (Szerszynski 1999: 211–13). In his attempts to understand what he terms the 'semiotic excess' of meaning in direct action protests, he shows how a new way of performing in the public domain had emerged in the 1990s. This was more pluralistic, even antagonistic, and in its symbolism more polysemic and ironic than previously. So aside from examining the attire of politicians, national dress and state leaders, this chapter concerns itself with public protest and assertive street dressing. This extends the discussion more broadly into ways in which dress and bodily display, as a specularisation of the political, functions dynamically at the heart of present-day street politics, thereby acting as symbolic instruments of transformation in the political process itself (Parkins 2002: 3).

Religious friction in Afghanistan and Kashmir, and dress prohibitions linked to repression, are notable instances of the transforming political affects of clothing practices. It is patently evident that there is no clearer way to grasp the nature of fundamentalism than to observe the rigid, exclusionary clothing laws of the Taliban in Afghanistan. They impose strict obligations for women to wear the full body covering, the *burqa*, with gauze patches over the eyes to block peripheral vision.[4] In 2001, a further Taliban edict forced minority Hindus to wear yellow cloth badges on shirt pockets, thus resurrecting a medieval European practice for identifying Jews (Farrell 2001: 7). Similarly in the same year the militant Kashmir group, Lashkar-e-Jabbar, sprayed acid on Muslim women, and threatened to shoot those refusing to wear the veil (*Australian* 2001: 20). Here the power of the privileged and/or socially strong is activated against the weak, marking a potent symbol of politics at work through the medium of dress.

It is surely one of our basic human rights to be able to wear the clothing of one's choice, yet it is sometimes the case that citizens are denied that privilege. For instance the Pentagon requires all female US Air Force personnel in Saudi Arabia, but not the men, to follow Muslim clothing restrictions. The requirement states that in day-to-day dealings with Arabs outside the base, women must wear a black headscarf and the full Muslim black robe or *abaya* (Kay 2002: 8). The US Air Force claims such dress is necessary to make female personnel less obvious to terrorists (Peek 2001). Lt Colonel Martha McSally, America's first and top woman combat fighter pilot, has legally challenged the Pentagon, speaking out vehemently about the requirement on cultural and religious grounds. Something of a gendered debate has ensued about institutional disrespect shown to US service women, and their inherent right to wear the dress of their own culture.[5] So military uniforms and civic clothing of all kinds, are types of dress whose embodied functions are embedded in the microprocesses of the state. They are intrinsic to the operations of institutional power, and are indicative of the ways dress functions in the formulation of gender differences.

Yet in the post 1980s world, bodily practices encoded through clothes are put to use as much in the enactment of relations of power as in those of resistance. So running counter to the imposition of uniforms is the unofficial camouflage dress of rebel fighters, in the jungles of Indonesia and elsewhere, or even the militia in Palestine. They do not wear regulation military dress although they appear militarised. They also resist the everyday civic clothing of their peers. This is a deliberate strategy to engender fear in opponents by using dress as a marker of political struggle. Yet uniforms, or pseudo uniforms are not the primary concern of this chapter. Even so, as agents of history these different but related categories of uniformly shaped and dressed body are part and parcel of the ways any society or group seeks to gain influence or to maintain power and political efficacy.

There can be little doubt clothing is implicated in the functioning of political structures at every level of social practice. Discussing the power and knowledge of relationships, working practices and operational modes of daily life, De Certeau proposes certain populist interventions into the hierarchies defined by the systems of the dominant in society. He suggests that we distinguish on a social level between what he calls strategies and tactics. Strategies are those more calculated, rational, even technocratic ways in which space is organised. They refer to the constraints of each social level, locating the subject and ways of functioning in a defined sense in relation to a particular place or activity. On the other hand tactics are the more opportunistic and mobile activities of the common people, lacking 'proper' or official locus. Tactics take advantage of, and play with, the 'space' delimited by others, much like a vigilant seizing of the moment. A tactic, he claims, is the art and activity of the weak in society (De Certeau 1984: 36–7). The differences in social practice to which he points, go some way to illuminate some of the variable functionings of political dress within the global arena.

One could argue that De Certeau's theories are too dichotomised to account fully for the precise functioning of the political messages of dress. For instance tactics, or 'spin', are not just employed by the socially weak, but also come within the dress practices of the dominant and politically powerful. These theoretical limitations are further demonstrated by the ways we can link the politics of dress and its visible meanings to recent changes in the relationship between culture and economics. Ray and Sayer have termed this factor the 'cultural turn', which they identify as a striking feature of the social and political landscape in the 1990s, and which they show to be beyond dialectical struggles between dominant and subordinate. This new climate reflected a shift from the former 'politics of distribution' focused on material resources, to a new aestheticised and more deeply culturalised 'politics of recognition'. This has been by no means restricted to the post-welfare capitalist world, but is in evidence far more widely (Ray and Sayer 1999: 18–19). In this 'turn' of events, in a thoroughly commodified and media directed culture, appearances, 'affect' and self presentation are given more weighting in public life than morality, social class and ability (Ray and Sayer 1999: 67). Subscribing to this theory, we must accept that even at the level of style, dress and its deployment is inevitably implicated in global political manoeuvrings, as well as more local strategising. We must also agree that a wide mix of imperatives constitutes the politics of dress.

Politicians

One of the evident conclusions in any study of global dress, is that all bodily covering and adornment impinges on the political, either directly or indirectly. Here it might be useful to bear in mind De Certeau's model that differentiates between strategies and tactics as we approach different ways to read clothing as political. One of the most formalised strategies of the socially powerful is the dress used both by male and female politicians, by and large favouring the business suit as an authoritative form of clothing. Public life depends to a great degree on reassurance given by an impersonal, serious code of dressing. Although, as Sennett shows, this does not mean appearances are, as a result, any less important or less meaningful (Sennett 1977: 161). Photographs of political figures and officials reaching some form of political agreement are a commonplace of media reporting. At such stage-managed events, be it in Brussels, Moscow or Beijing, it is usual to see groups, mostly of men, gathered to mark the event. Engaging in the symbolic handshake of agreement, they all wear quite similar, dark coloured suits. Their clothing conforms to what one might call a recognisable schema made up of reassuring and predictable ingredients.

But within this superficially uniform schema, politicians do display subtly differentiated personal tastes and styles. This complies with Sennett's hypothesis about city life in which the drab, uniform-like public dress (he is writing of Victorian men) creates a form of shield, ostensibly to play down their personal differences. But in terms of individuality, what actually happens is quite the reverse. Dull, uniform clothes have the effect of demanding the viewer look far more attentively and to decode their micro details to detect signs of character, psychological difference and social position (Sennett 1977: 165–6). On the other hand, dress worn by politicians and officials in non-western cultures can contradict the subtle decoding demanded by this kind of attire. Overtly symbolic accessories sometimes mark out religious and national differences that may seem incongruous to western eyes. Suits can, for instance, be worn in conjunction with traditional or religious dress, such as the Jewish skullcap the *kippah* or *yarmulke*. In Fiji there is a custom of wearing the tailored suit jacket with a cloth skirt-like garment, the *sulu vakataga*.

Suits of course have gendered implications. Suit wearing for women, in this context those worn by women politicians, has different connotations from that of their male counterparts, carrying sexually contradictory messages; according to Entwistle the jacket tends to diminish sexuality and the skirt enhance it (Entwistle 2000a: 190). Embedded in the notion of dressing for success, the suit is implicated in the struggle women have had for political and sexual liberation particularly since the 1970s (Benstock and Ferriss 1994: 5). The US powerbroker, former Secretary of State Madeleine Albright, used the suit as a primary article of her wardrobe, her jacket blending with her male colleagues as she negotiated around the board table, her skirt visible only when inspecting facilities and for photo calls. But she personalised and enlivened suits with striking pieces of costume jewellery, brooches and necklaces, eloquently demonstrating that ornamentation could be an aesthetic taste but also symbolic of official status. Strictly speaking one cannot describe her use of clothes as political gestures. Yet the clear message of her dress was to signal her power (as a messenger of the US government) whose significance was not merely a matter of gender.

Entwistle argues that 'power dressing' offers dress principles for professional women but does not address the widespread inequalities of women in the workforce. It simply reproduces the conventional notions that women should manage their sexuality (Entwistle 2000b: 237). Yet there is a further point about suit wearing by someone like Albright. As a political figure with high visibility, she used suits as a strategy to further her own agenda, rather than simply to manage her femininity. Thus, her clothes and those of other political women like her, act as exemplars for strengthening women's position in the higher echelons of power. An interesting contrast to Albright might be the Indonesian President, Megawati Sukarnoputri. Like many of her female compatriots, she has taken the decision to wear national dress or *kebaya national* on official occasions. In its various permutations, it can be either the Javanese *kain dan kebaya panjang* or the Sumatran *sarung dan kebaya panjang*, sometimes with a *selendang* or *tundung* which is a headscarf. Such references, either to Javanese or Sumatran tradition, function visibly and deliberately as a public sign of national inclusiveness.[6]

Politicians are acutely aware of the importance of their clothed appearances. Within the parameters of mainstream clothing, many have been advised to change their 'looks' by image consultants and 'spin doctors', thereby acknowledging their personal style of dress has important ramifications at the ballot box. But there are political leaders whose interest and use of dress is especially distinctive, sometimes conciliatory. One noted example is the clothing of Hamid Karzai, the interim President of the new Afghanistan, a Pashtun from the south. He has carefully chosen an inclusive wardrobe that combines tunics and loose trousers, typical of rural Afghanistan, sometimes double breasted blazers as a gesture to the west, a flat

12 Nelson Mandela in a 'Madiba' shirt, meeting with Yasser Arafat in his recognisable *kaffiyeh* in 2000

peaked karakul hat and at times a purple and emerald cape or *chapan*, the latter two types of garment typical of the northern Tajik and Uzbek tribes. (Jackson 2002: 12). Yasser Arafat is another distinctive dresser, with his trademark Saudi or Syrian style *kaffiyeh* of white and black checked fabric.[7] This he has worn consistently for twenty years, together with khaki military duds, suggesting he is on a war footing at all times. He is seen here (Figure 12) meeting Nelson Mandela, a political figure, as we have seen, who has also shown a deliberate understanding of the important role that dress symbolism can play within the political process. Mandela's associates have testified to his meticulous attention to the details of his appearance and, since he was a young man, a desire to be the 'best dressed'.[8]

In the early 1990s Mandela began to adopt his signature style, the characteristic, long-sleeved 'Madiba' shirt. It is made from either patterned cotton or silk, the name deriving from his traditional clan. Part of a carefully calculated political image, the shirt has striking similarities to batik patterned shirts worn in Indonesia. There are conflicting accounts of the outfit's origin. One source claims the idea came from Yusuf Surtie, the son of Mandela's first tailor, who based it on the leader's liking for Suharto's shirts that he saw during a trip to Indonesia in 1992 (Schouten 1999: 1).[9] Another source credits Sonwabile Ndamase, first president of the South African Fashion Designers Association, with the idea long before Mandela became President (Mofokeng 1999: 1).[10] The intriguing thing about this shirt is that it is quite different from normal shirts worn with western style tailored suits. Rather it seems a relaxed, leisurely garment, a popular style with which the people can have sympathy. This constellation of meanings has suited the widely admired leader extremely well, and sits with the warm hearted, elder statesman image he has cultivated in his later years.

Although it looks similar to the Indonesian batik shirt, widely worn by Indonesian government officials including former President Abdurrahman Wahid, the 'Madiba' shirt has become symbolic of Mandela's South Africa. Similar garments are widely sold as tourist souvenirs for both sexes in South Africa, and also for sportswear.[11] Its meanings have thus multiplied. In an interesting twist the *East African* weekly paper noted in October 1998 that the 'Madiba' shirt was being feverishly embraced by Tanzanian men of all walks of life.[12] The reasons for this are not entirely clear, but the shirt may signify a form of widespread, fairly unspecific African solidarity, or may make a point about Africa's colourful and supposedly leisurely approach to dressing in comparison to Europe.

Yet in another sense the shirt transcends specific cultures. It is a garment whose meanings function unequally, moving in and out of the commodity state, in what Appadurai calls 'different regimes of value', registered both spatially and in time. Although these regimes are unevenly weighted, even in its 'commodity phase', the shirt is loaded with political meanings (Appadurai 1986: 4 and 11). This is made evident by the fact that 'Madiba' shirts are popular commodities, but they have also served as symbolic gift exchanges within an entirely different register of values. 'Madiba' shirts, Indonesian batik shirts, and indeed Chinese garments such as silk jackets, have been used as tokens, given by host countries to international dignitaries at important meetings and events, including CHOGM and APEC (Asia-Pacific Economic Co-operation) gatherings.[13] These intercultural garment exchanges and displays take place outside normal and customary circuits.[14] Used as a sign of political solidarity and friendship, their value is thus enhanced, putting them well beyond the everyday (Appadurai 1986: 28).

The meanings of the Arafat *kaffiyeh* have been expanded in a somewhat similar fashion to the 'Madiba' shirt, but are complicated by ongoing political controversies in the Middle East. Initially worn as a sign of Palestinian sympathy, by the end of the 1980s they were becoming instead fashionable scarves. Adopted by women and men, they were a youthful street style, almost as popular as running shoes and fatigue jackets. Cocks suggest that an informal poll conducted by the interim director of the Chicago-based Palestinian Human Rights Campaign found that only three out of ten people mentioned politics as the reason for wearing the scarves – '"It is just an accessory" says Kenneth Kaiser, a Boston retail clothing-store manager. "The ethnic type of look is in right now"' (Cocks 1988: 72). The garment's original political meanings had thus become debased, shifting to fashionable 'ethnic' chic, leisure wear and tourist souvenirs. So at that time its use by everyday consumers folded back any of its original meanings, thus making the garment merely an example of stylish dress. With accelerated difficulties that have emerged between Jews and Palestinians in the Middle East, the original politicised meanings of *kaffiyeh* wearing seem to have been reactivated.

Dress, politics and the media

It would not be a generalisation to say that the mass media is increasingly obsessed with image, and with the dress style of politicians as political indicators. Both the media and the public appear to take more interest in the appearance of women politicians than they do of men, but unquestionably both sexes come in for attention within the political arena. For instance, in 1999, everyday, casual jeans became a site of contestation in the Italian parliament when female legislators wore them in an inappropriate context to protest against the Supreme Court of Appeals ruling that women cannot be raped in these garments (Parkins 2002: 1). For many years lawyers have hired fashion consultants to evaluate their client's 'looks' prior to a trial. O. J. Simpson, for instance, was asked to choose a highly respectful corporate wardrobe of dark grey and blue suits with crisp white shirts to gain juror sympathy in his pre-trial hearings (Johnson 1994: 108). This acknowledgement that dress can sway opinions has important implications for anyone in the public eye. Clearly public and press obsession with appearance means politicians are impelled to pay more and more attention to the way they dress. If the courtroom is a dramatic stage, how much more significant then is the global, politica! stage.

But can hairstyles and clothing win elections? Does style ever substitute for policy? In April 2001, Junichiro Koizumi became the twenty-seventh postwar Prime Minister of Japan, the world's second largest economy. Riding on the platform of 'Change the LDP. Change Japan', the shaggy, long haired Koizumi appeared to observers to have specifically cultivated an unkempt appearance in keeping with his desire to be an 'oddball' maverick, but new style reformer. Wearing light suits, uncharacteristic for

Japanese men, his long, wavy hairstyle curls just above his shirt collar. Journalists claimed his clothing was a deliberate attempt to appeal to younger voters, suspicious of the slicked-down coiffure of the politicians they felt had let them down (Lunn 2001: 6). At the time of his election, Aides feared the permanent wave (said to be the first in the Japanese Diet) could lose him votes, since its overt stylishness might slip over into untrustworthiness (Lunn 2001: 13). This did not happen and he won hands down, able to maintain that crucial and delicate balance between style and credibility.

Koizumi's capability may not have been such an isolated case. With its major shifts in economic and social policy Britain's New Labour, successful in the 1997 General Election, showed the skilful and modernised embrace of presentation. It did this under the able tutelage of the party's 'spin doctors', led by Alistair Campbell, Blair's Press Secretary (Driver and Martell 1999: 262). Interestingly, in an article written for the *New Statesman* the following year, Melanie McDonagh argued that a paradox had emerged in New Labour, between the party's rhetoric about new and modern policy directions and what she saw as party requirements to conform to 'herd instinct' or corporate dressing. Moreover, the widespread view that Labour's win was a victory of style over substance was in fact, she suggests, not evident in their clothes with the possible exceptions of Tony and Cherie Blair, John Prescott and Peter Mandelson (McDonagh 1998: 1–2).[15]

Interestingly the dress of male politicians' wives has traditionally attracted media attention, perhaps even more than that of their husbands, from Jackie Kennedy's cool French style elegance to Nancy Reagan's conspicuous consumption. Many politicians' wives have been able to use fashion extremely efficaciously to support their husbands and to promote their nation's fashion industry. What is important is that the use of fashion in this way has manifested itself with great variety. Hillary Clinton, for instance, showed unease with fashion after her husband's presidential election. Her interests seemed to have been more with health care than couture. Despite her preference for lawyerly business suits, she frequently changed her hairstyles. 'If we ever want to get Bosnia off the front page, she once complained, all I have to do is change my hair' (*People's Weekly* 1993: 1).

Nationalism and dress

In as much as dress can be in the forefront of politics in the developed world, clothing has had a large part to play in the establishment and ongoing social practices of new nations. In the aftermath of post World War II economic and political upheavals, about one hundred new nations were formed, each concerned in some way with rewriting or re-establishing their past (Childs and Williams 1997: 209). Many used clothing in an overtly strategic manner towards this re-establishment. For instance the voluntary wearing of uniforms, to signal freedom from past oppressions, during the cleansing period in Indonesia that accompanied the rise of Suharto (Nordholt 1997: 25). Or the appropriation of the Chinese Mao suit by Tanzania revolutionaries, and indeed by Julius Nyerere himself.

In the wake of colonialism, and as a result of the insecurities brought about by globalisation, many newly forming nations officially endorsed certain modified forms of customary or ethnic dress they felt best represented their specific cultural character, authenticity and traditions. Importantly publicly endorsed national forms of dress have continued to coexist with western dress in various permutations. As well, tactical struggles that surround national claims and debates about progress can include practices of dress even at grassroots levels. Examining politics alone without understanding the crucial role played by dress in the formation of new nations in the aftermath of colonialism is to see only part of the picture. Fandy's important account of dress and spatiality in Egypt, for example, shows quite explicitly that if we study Egyptian politics without attending to the complexity and multiplicity of its dress styles, we gain a false impression of the state as centralised. Dress actually undermines the received view that Egypt is homogenous. In other words if we ignore clothing in Egypt, we fail to see the dynamic relations and tensions, the strategies and enactments, as they operate between those parts of the country clinging to traditional attire and those more westernised (Fandy 1998: 5).

Dress has been one of the west's most 'successful' legacies to the rest of the world, especially so with men's attire. Initially imposed by colonial governments and missionaries keen on assimilation, western style shirts, trousers, skirts and jackets are voluntarily worn everywhere in newly formed, independent nations from the Philippines and New Guinea, to India and Africa. Yet these clothes have not always been accepted or even welcomed by new nations, although their encroachment has been insidious. New nations sometimes symbolically stage a quasi-ritualised rejection of western civilisation and its attire in an attempt to assert political strengths. Witness the Mau Mau freedom fighters in Kenya who deliberately took the *Batuni* oath of allegiance naked (Mazrui 1970: 27). Alternatively indigenous or other dress is often spontaneously adopted as an important indicator of nationalist sentiment, and as a popular form of grassroots response.

On the other hand, there are ways in which post-colonial societies and nations perform their traditional culture in a kind of border zone or mutually acceptable space of identity. They do this not so much for themselves but more often on behalf of the tourist. Malaysia showcases stereotypical distillations of traditional dress in cultural performances and dances that are acceptably contained, offering to the tourist suitably non-threatening forms of national diversity and multicultural tolerance (Cunningham 1998: 88). This show of nationhood belies the ethnic minorities in Malaysia, who are disparate, non-harmonious and eager to subvert the official government message. There are other similar examples. Hawaii is an instance of what Friedman calls the 'polycentrism of identity formation', straddled between a tourist industry keen to stage old style Hawaiianess in order to sell the nostalgic 'plantation' image to visitors, and the grassroots Hawaiian movement that opposes this (Friedman 1994: 181). Here one finds a doubling of the meanings in dress where the reinstating of a form of past attire, or even as a memorialising of the past, accompanies an expression of the national present.

But as with all kinds of clothing, unless laws are enacted and enforced, dress coercion seldom works. In many new nations the introduction of so called national dress has been partial, fragmented and sometimes artificially conceived. An example is the self-conscious use and promotion of a national dress for men and women during the Philippine Centenary celebrations 1996–98, one hundred years after revolution from Spanish rule. During this period workers in government offices were required to wear national clothing on Mondays, the transparent *barong tagalog* shirt for men and the *baro't saya* for women. The latter is a thin blouse and long skirt modified from the starched *terno* of formal nationalist dress for women. Both male and female dress was popularly termed Filipiniana, or Centennial dress, that is it referred to a contrived costume. This was ironically based on colonial dress, but sufficiently altered to suit busy office workers and acceptable to those with anti-colonial sentiments (Labrador 1999: 59).

Finding a politically appropriate national dress for men in African countries, with suitable links to tradition, has proved especially problematic, given they went almost naked in tribal society. Politicians have variously called for attire that will suit new nation status both in Uganda and Kenya, where no national dress exists.[16] For much of the Nyerere era, the problem was solved by the Mao suit, then the collarless *kiMao* and subsequently the Zambian Kaunda or safari suit, all de facto official dress for men. Even in the later 1990s, the western suit rubbed shoulders with the *kiMao* and the *Kaunda* in the National Assembly (*East African Weekly* 1998: 19–25).

A somewhat similar problem was resolved by the Indonesians after 1965–66 and the rise of the Suharto New Order government. Safari suits, originally designed as leisure suits for use in India and Africa, were introduced as the formal dress for government officials instead of business suits (Sekimoto 1997: 317). Since the 1970s, government officials have replaced

suits with the long sleeved batik shirt for formal occasions, banquets and
receptions and unlike the informal short-sleeved shirt, it must have three
pockets. (van Dijk 1997: 73). Batik of the same design can be used to signal
different organisational and even political groupings, including the use of
yellow by the Golkar Party. These shirts are worn with the nationalist black
peci cap, tall for high ranking civil servants and small for those lower in
rank (Danandjaja 1997: 257). This group of government officials and clerks,
chatting on the Muslim day of rest at Ramarinda in the province of
Kalimantan, wear the *peci*, as well as white prayer caps, and batik shirts
(Figure 13). President Sukarno appropriated the *peci* cap from the 'common
Malay worker' in the 1920s. It thus symbolised freedom, national ideals
and indigenous style, in contrast to imposed western dress (van Dijk 1997:
70–1). President Wahid continued the practice of wearing the *peci*, as did
many of his ministers, as a deliberate way of elevating worker clothing to
the level of national symbol. (Further discussion on hats and their global
meanings can be found in chapter 6.)

It is commonly believed that national dress is a relatively static form

13 Government officials and clerks on a Friday morning in 1992 at Ramarinda,
Kalimantan. They are wearing *peci* and other white caps, and formal shirts made
from batik fabric

of attire and symbolic of the state. But national dress is not a 'frozen' style, nor is it necessarily an 'official' style, although it can be generated by the nation's politically educated, urban elite (Taylor 2002: 213). All the evidence points to it being quite mutable, and it can be a social agreement to wear a form of dress, rather than an imposition. The reclamation of the Scottish kilt as a socially radical form of dress, rather than sign of the elite in the 1990s, is a case in point (Taylor 2002: 220). Indeed the homogeneity and consensus that nationalism wishes to promote, does not necessarily match with a corresponding and completely unified clothing discourse. One of the reasons is that nationalism tries simultaneously to represent itself as forward looking, but at the same time to reaffirm traditional cultural practices and collective customs (Childs and Williams 1997: 205).

But there is a further point. So called national style is often deployed for commercial benefits. Governments see advantage in linking nationalist iconography with commodities, as a way of boosting the tourist market. In Australia the T-shirt market, to take an example, began to boom in the early 1970s, in tandem with an expansion of leisure activities. But this growing market was also a direct result of the government's push to encourage local products with Australiana or nationalistic motifs, to assist an ailing fashion and clothing industry. It was also part of jingoism at the time of the Commonwealth Games held in Brisbane in 1982 and the America's Cup Challenge race.

T-shirt sales, in fact, have been crucial to the Australian tourist trade, proving to be ideally suited to receiving not only Australiana or nationalist-type designs but imprints of indigenous motifs as well. As early as the end of the 1960s the Australian government and community agencies began seriously encouraging indigenous craftspeople to design textiles and make clothing, using supposedly 'authentic' motifs and colours, as a route toward self-sufficiency and cultural reclamation. Many indigenous design centres were set up about this time or earlier, such as Bima Wear and Tiwi Designs on Bathurst Island north of Darwin, and Ernabella in northwest South Australia, all producing distinctive T-shirts for the tourist market (Maynard 2000a: 149). Even after the 1970s, when many Aboriginal art centres came under indigenous control, a tourist marketing staple has been T-shirts and sarongs. These are garments easily able to display the designs and marks of Aboriginality, yet there are many problems associated with indigenous imagery on T-shirts for it does not fall into the same category as Australiana. The very popularity of indigenous T-shirt designs is synonymous with their capacity for exploitation, hence their politicised nature. As mass produced garments they are also easy to reproduce, but also to copy without permission. For this reason mass produced T-shirts, with unauthenticated replica designs, marked a battle ground in the 1980s over indigenous ownership of design. This resulted finally in 1989 to entitlement to protection under the Copyright Act (Johnson 1996: 6). On one level these garments are marketed as 'authentically' Australian, but on another they are garments of resistance, and represent the equivalent of land right claims in fabric, thus key sites of Aboriginal struggle for autonomy over their own culture.

Dress for protest

Apart from national clothing that intentionally constructs ideas about the state, there is a further important aspect of political dressing, within the global arena, that sets it apart from mainstream clothing. This is dress worn at sites of political protest and street confrontation. One might regard this kind of clothing as fully tactical in De Certeau's terms. Where national clothing is often carefully and strategically shaped according to specific agendas, the clothing worn by political and economic protestors is subject to no controls or reservations, although it usually complies with certain predetermined schemas. According to customary social procedures in west-ern society, a fundamental part of the modern, so called civilising process, is the adoption of acceptable clothing codes, themselves linked to customary etiquette and behaviours. At direct action protests of various kinds, these codes are either deliberately transgressed or suspended.

Some of the most politicised of garments are inscribed T-shirts, and sweaters, worn by anti-nuclear and environmental protestors and indeed anti-globalisation protestors. Their meanings are often quite ephemeral. Like wall posters they can be produced in a matter of hours, and marketed to support momentary causes and express current ideas. They are a highly personal medium of communication in a world that seems to pay less and less heed to individual viewpoints. T-shirt wearers can engage with others in the public cultural arena, where subjective identities are perfor-mative and unfixed, an ideal theatre for these garments to play a political role. Supporters of the Tibetan Youth Congress in New Delhi in 2002 (Figure 14) are wearing red and yellow sweaters inscribed with slogans protesting at China's occupation of Tibet. The GAP shirt in the background, a sign of the global force of branded clothing, ironically features here at a protest rally. It is the very ephemerality of T-shirts that makes them difficult to locate and research, but equally pertinent to the everyday nature of political resistance.[17] There are also few in-depth studies of T-shirts as a medium of resistance, but they clearly play a significant role, signalling solidarity during acts of self-assertion, rebellion and disaffection. Goldman has recently shown that the wearing of printed T-shirts by Chicano students

14 Members of the Tibetan Youth Congress near the diplomatic enclave in New Delhi, 2002. They wear striped bandanas and their brightly coloured sweaters are inscribed with slogans supporting the withdrawal of China from Tibet

in Mexico was partly artistic expression but also an attempt to facilitate self-determination. The images on the shirts had a narrative content that was folkloric but they also had a political function. Goldman argues that the wearing of these shirts was a mark of resistance against Euro-American dominance, and was a politicised practice of affirmation, not simply a representation of ethnic pride (Goldman 1997: 125).

Similarly, in Australia, T-shirts worn by indigenous people, are deeply politicised garments. They have readily borne the inscriptions of resistance, especially since the early 1980s. Some of the earliest examples, in the black, red and yellow colours of the indigenous flag, were worn during marches organised by the Black Protest Committee during the 1982 Commonwealth Games in Brisbane, and to protest for Land Rights legislation (Watson 1988: 40). Important too were the schematic red, yellow and black shirts worn at events like the handover of title to Uluru (Ayers Rock) in 1985. T-shirts with their textual and other logos are proud statements of indigenous identity, and are a key part of Aboriginal political strategies to counter a colonial history of imposing covering on indigenous bodies.[18]

Anti-uranium mining, anti-logging and environmental protests of the 1970s and 1980s, on behalf of protest movements like Greenpeace, drew out particular instances of oppositional dressing, often marked by the wearing of didactic sloganised T-shirts. Protest T-shirts can be ideological markers, like the 'Dolphin Freedom' and 'Sanctuary' T-shirt, successfully retailed by Greenpeace in the mid-1990s. But the intensity of protest can fade and causes do evaporate. Questions remain as to whether 'Green' protest shirts are merely a successful marketing venture, even further confusing the meanings of these garments.

In the early twenty-first century economic protestors are of a slightly different order. Their protests centre on the belief that fewer and fewer large corporations are controlling what we eat, drink and wear. These opponents of globalisation are engaged in a new form of symbolic street drama, increasingly underwritten by the internet, and constituted fundamentally by a non-hierarchical and loose organisational format. They are thus prey to many different interests. Probably starting in 1996 with attempts to reclaim the streets and support striking Liverpool dockers (Wynhausen 2001: 31), the new forms of campaign are very complex. They are far less ideologically coherent, and directed toward 'effects' and punning rather than straightforward meaningfulness (Szerszynski 1999: 212). Within reason and practicality, one can wear what one pleases at these protests. Yet the air is mixed with a tension generated between protective gear, disposal shop gear, black and red anarchists scarves and the carnivalesque. The latter can be anything from mock funeral attire and face masks (Prague), to the dress of nuns in dark glasses and back packs or nature lovers in turtle suits (Seattle).

Protestors who have access to the internet can log onto 'Survival Guide' information about what to wear. Participants at the S11 WEF Protest, in September 2000 in Melbourne, were advised to bring gas masks, helmets and goggles, a change of clothing, pants and shirt, to replace clothing contaminated by teargas and kneepads for kneeling on hard roads. They were to wear no earrings, have no piercings, necklaces or ties. Windcheaters and light rain gear were for inclement weather and for camouflage. The 'Prague 2000 Survival Guide' had an 'Action Fashion' section and an 'Action Fashion Faux Pas' section.[19] The recommendations were for comfortable protective shoes, protective clothes from sun and pepper spray, protective eyewear, such as goggles or sunglasses, damp bandanas, heavy duty gloves and cap or hat to protect from sun and chemical weapons. The 'Faux Pas' section advised against sun screens and Vaseline that traps chemicals, dangling jewellery and long hair.

In the global arena the enacted forms of change, as expressed by dress, firstly address, and then redress, the wearers' experiences of the social condition. This occurs as individuals or groups move from one set of social circumstances to another, or as they encounter and re-encounter one another in daily life. All these changes have quite complex and deep-seated ramifications for the politics of clothing, especially as dress is deeply embedded in religious and ethnic claims about national and minority identity, as well as personal belief systems. But more than this, the material nature of clothes, their colours, shapes, and how they are variously chosen, evaluated and consumed, have complex and tangible effects on, and are the result of social and cultural interactions. The latter themselves are subject to political decisions and relations of power, to the precise locale and of course the causes of the day.

Choices to make about what to wear (or fail to be allowed to make), the access we have to goods, and the information we convey to others determine, but can also arise from, our particular social circumstances. These factors in turn are linked to economic situations and to political decisions made on our behalf. Whether we are talking about protest clothing, the clothing of new nations or the dress of high profile politicians, attire and self-presentation lies at the heart of much political strategy formulation. As the role of the citizen is remade in the resurgence of national cultures after colonialism, or as youthful protestors signal their disaffection with the activities of global corporate giants, we find that clothing of the self is implicated in one way or another. It is impossible to consider dress and globalisation without attending to the manifold examples of the political at work.

Notes

1 Mandela is a member of the Madiba clan of the Thembu people of the South African region of the Transkei.

2 On her first public appearance in 1962, replacing her husband then in prison, she opened the Indian Youth Congress Conference in Johannesburg draped in a yellow sari, allowing the young Indians to festoon her body in yellow carnations (Meer 1990: 208–9). On this occasion she used dress to signal sympathy with Indians, a similarly oppressed people in South Africa.

3 A *hanbok* consists of *ch'ima* (full-length skirt) and *chogo*ri (short dress jacket) (Soh 1992: 76).

4 The Taliban made it illegal for women to wear make-up, nail polish, any stylish clothes, sheer stockings or even high heels.

5 See the anonymous website entitled 'Why Major Martha McSally is wrong' which offers the non-western perspective. It claims the *abaya* is not Islamic but part of the religion and culture of Wahabbism, the foundation religion of the Saudi state. To wear this clothing is courtesy to the host nation. www.geocities.com/wshinglaton/sopabox23april2001.html.

6 My thanks to the Embassy of the Republic of Indonesia, Canberra, for this information.

7 This headcloth, sometimes spelled *kaffiyah, ghutrah* or *shmāgh*, is worn with an *agāl* rope. (Yamani 1997: 45).

8 Perhaps more significant was his appearance at the 1962 Pretoria Trial. He deliberately appeared in court in a dramatic and traditional jackal skin kaross, his fellow
clan members also attended in traditional dress, and bore ceremonial weaponry of
sticks. Mandela was ordered to remove the kaross, as white officials feared that the
sight of it would rouse tribal feelings among other prisoners, but he refused to do
so and it remained on his body for the whole trial (Meer 1990: 211).

9 G. Schouten, 'Just a change of clothes', 15 June 1999. www.vnw.nl/hotspots/archive/
zaf/html/southafrica150699.html.

10 L. Mofokeng, 'He made Madiba shirts a cut above the rest', 11 July 1999, www.sunday
times.co.za/1999/07/11arts/gauteng/aneg07.htm.

11 An example of a long-sleeved 'Madiba' shirt, is manufactured with short sleeves by
the Nuance Golf Inc., Utah, US, as part of their Safari Golf Apparel range.

12 *East African Weekly*, 'Not Suitable for Tanzania?', 19–25 October 1998. http://www
.nationaudio.com/News/EastAfrican/1910/Opinion/Opinion10.html.

13 Mandela is known to have given a 'Madiba' shirt to both President Clinton and
to Kofi Annan. At the APEC 2001 meeting in Beijing, President Bush was given a
mandarin style jacket by his Chinese hosts.

14 Eicher cites an interesting instance of the way in which President Clinton's dress
advisers allowed him to misunderstand Indonesian presentation batik shirts as
casual dress at the APEC Forum in 1994, rather than as formal wear which is their
correct meaning (Eicher *et al.* 2000: 43).

15 Blair himself was advised by Malcolm Levine, a tailor used by the movie world,
and also by the firm Paul Smith.

16 In Uganda, Major General Elly Tumwine, since student days a keen opponent of
western dress, initiated the so-called Tumwine suit for wear in Parliament, a sleeveless
coat of cotton that can be worn with a long-sleeved shirt and tie (*Africa News
Service* 1999: 2), InfoTrac.

17 Howard Besser's T-shirt database http://sunsite.berkeley.edu/T-Shirts/ is therefore a
useful, constantly updated photographic archive of these garments, cataloguing a
vast range of shirts worn at alternative venues by anarchists, anti-nuclear activists,
environmental protesters and so on.

18 For a detailed discussion of this issue see Maynard (2002).

19 www.urban75.com/Action/s2603html, accessed July 2001.

4 ✧ Ethnic dress or fashionably 'ethnic'?

This collective style depends on specific sociological conditions, ones that are increasingly unfulfilled as Muria society becomes differentiated. As time goes by they will cease to dress as Muria, but will *dress up* as Muria when making explicit their ethnicity, heretofore implicit. (Gell 1986)

ALTHOUGH one cannot deny that in many parts of the world traditional customary dress is being swallowed up at variously different rates with the invasiveness of western culture, ethnicity as expressed in dress remains an important, if complicated, factor within globalisation. The developed world has tended to typecast ethnicity as its stable opposite, worthy of appropriation but beyond fashionable change (Eicher 1995: 300). This creates a false aesthetic boundary around ethnic style, one that allows the west to imagine it inevitably declining under the impact of modern progress, or alternatively to raid its range of exotic delights and secure them firmly within the western frame. Although ethnicity is a problematic term that presupposes a western viewpoint, if we wish to define 'ethnic' dress, it is more appropriate to regard it as part of day-to-day cultural transactions and connectedness. This recognises that ethnic identity is not discrete or firmly fixed, but about a wider and constantly changing set of meanings, collective and individual, 'externalised in social interaction and internalised in personal self-identification' (Jenkins 1997: 165).

Yet, as Jenkins warns, there is more to difference than the fact of diversity. Even though ethnic identity is transactional and changeable, available for appropriation or even resistant, it does not mean it always is, or that it has to be so. Ethnicity can be more, or indeed less, flexible in different places and at different times (Jenkins 1997: 51). Accepting this, one of the issues to consider is the way in which the particularity of ethnicity simultaneously interacts with the apparent homogeneity of global dress, something whose consensual 'sameness' is equally subject to question. So are local or subgroup differences in dress ever fully obliterated within the depthlessness of the globalising process, or do they survive in new ways through accommodation, by exploitation or through repackaging and reuse (Robins 1991: 33)? We might also ask if customary dress can itself originate in the attire of another culture. We have the case of the Muria of Madhya Pradesh in India whose dress and definition of clothing prestige is adopted from outsiders. Lacking their own authentic style, they take on the fashion of Hindus with whom they trade; their cloth and jewellery all closely associated with those who are non-Muria (Gell 1986: 120–2).

These are intricate issues, particularly as the circumstances in which we find ethnicity expressed in everyday western style clothing are remarkably extensive. For instance, high fashion and indeed the mass market persistently consumes enlivening exotic features and elements borrowed from the customary dress of others. Furthermore, 'ethnic' dress of various types has inspired much urban subcultural clothing since the 1960s, and 'alternative' dress has also drawn many ideas from the supposed 'genuineness' of non-western textile designs, jewellery and body modifications. Tourist industries all over the world feed a voracious souvenir market by offering what is claimed to be 'authentic' ethnic clothing, and by fabricating indigenous style dress and textiles. But there is little evidence of how those whose traditions are exploited respond to appropriation. An exception is the work of Puwar centred on South Asian women in the UK, who themselves partake of exoticised clothing consumption. She shows that these women respond differently from British consumers with a white heritage. They feel mixed emotions, including anxiety, and even rage, about wholesale and packaged fantasising of Asian culture, which for them remains historically uncontextualised (Puwar 2002: 63 and 82).

To complicate the issue further there are numerous indigenous communities where customary clothing has been hybridised with dress common to the developed world. In Eastern Indonesia, western styles can be made up using indigenous *ikat* textiles, thereby creating a truly hybrid style. Although there is fairly indiscriminate use of textiles belonging to regions other than that of the wearer, this de-emphasises former regional diversity in favour of a new, politically desirable ethnic homogeneity (Molnar 1998: 54–5). Cuna Indian children in Panama and Colombia, expected to wear western school clothing, defiantly decorate it with traditional cut out appliqué *molas* also making their dress fully hybrid (Herald 1992: 161–2).[1] But there are many other cases, including Indonesia, where clothing of two cultures are both used, either separately or in combination, on different occasions or for different purposes and to achieve different results. We see this illustrated by young men of Cajas, Department of Piura, northern

15 A group of young Cajas men, Department of Piura, northern Peru, 2000 clad in Andean regional wool ponchos and leather hats, combined with various forms of western clothing

Peru, photographed in 2000 (Figure 15) who wear both customary-style Andean regional ponchos of wool and broad-brimmed leather hats, and modern western type baseball caps, trousers, windcheaters and gumboots seemingly for reasons of practicality.

Such complications make evident that there is no habitual way of defining 'ethnic' dress, nor can it be expressed in terms of stasis. In fact 'ethnic' or customary clothes can exhibit a constant preoccupation with novelty, much like western fashion. Indigenous Yoruba *aso-oke* and *adire* cloth is used to make up fashionable clothes but its designers also treat it as responsively as fashion, constantly changing and adapting designs with new motifs, new yarns and new ideas (Perani and Wolff 1999: 174–7). Printed Ghanaian *Adinkra* cloth, with its changing meanings and narratives, follows a similar path. Nor should we think of customary dress as homogeneous. Islamic dress is a case in point. In Egypt clothing, that might at first appear ethnically similar, is quite the reverse. It is composed of many regional Islamic styles, divided between urban and rural populations, between elite and non-elite, north and south and of course between men and women (Fandy 1998: 5). In Bouake, Côte d'Ivoire, there are three major styles in local women's dress, Muslim, African and western inspired. But even these break down into a number of subsets based on social or professional status, or specific identities that include what LeBlanc terms 'Arabised Muslim' attire, that is influenced by Kuwait and Saudi Arabia (LeBlanc 2000: 449–50).

Beyond internal subtleties, as much geographical as racial, religious or social, many additional types of relationship exist between different kinds of global dress and various forms of 'ethnic' dress worn all over the world. In the 1980s, the Laotian Hmong, refugees from the Vietnam War, who now live in Minnesota (see chapter 6), abandoned their former customary dress on ceremonial occasions, creating instead a new 'ethnic' group identity in their clothing (Lynch 1995: 262). So customary and western everyday dress are constantly in various forms of dynamic relation one to another. But it is not simply a case of confusion. Mustafa, discussing African styles of clothing in Dakar, coins the phrase 'sartorial ecumenes' to describe what are the specific and local lexicons which revolve around a dichotomy between traditional /African and European / *tubaab*, that is foreign attire (Mustafa 1998: 22 and 31).[2]

The vast proliferation of ethnic minorities, regional, national and transnational communities is an acknowledged fact of globalisation (Kegley and Wittkopf 2001a: 175). The 1980s and 1990s witnessed an upsurge in nationalist separatism, migration and the turmoil of changing ethnopolitical groupings and sectional interests. In the latter half of the twentieth century unprecedented movements of population across frontiers took place and continue to do so. As different ethnic groups migrate, or come together for various reasons, they maintain certain established practices of attire, but at the same time find difficulty in sustaining absolutely separate forms of clothing in new environments. As part of mutation within diasporic migrations and shifts, ethnic identities in new countries have been shown not to mirror precisely practices in the homeland, rather using a range of sources to shape new ways of doing things. Noble's study of Arab-speaking youth living in the South Western areas of Sydney, for instance, shows how identity formation moves between essentialism – their given ethnicity – and a strategic hybridity of elements drawn both from the parent culture and participation in Australian society (Noble *et al.* 1999: 29). He found youths moved positionally between stereotypical ethnicity and an apparent unconcern with issues of ethnic display. Noble regarded this as a sign of possessing a repertoire of socially useful subject positions, that could be used in different contexts (Noble *et al.* 1999: 40). So we might say that there are ethnic groups whose identity is constituted by an asserted cohesiveness. Yet their subjectivity and indeed appearances are simultaneously subject to alteration, as they actively enter new social and spatial configurations, and respond to contact with others (Noble *et al.* 1999: 30).

Ethnicity is clearly part of a system of responses, something quite mutable, in which groups and individuals occupy both their own place, as well as impinging on others and related spaces beyond.

Appadurai, in his theorising about irregular and disjunctive flows within the global arena, proffers a conceptualisation of such workings of complex relations between groups, villages, and neighbourhoods both real and imaginary. These he terms 'ethnoscapes', defined as a constantly moving and complicated landscape of persons, tourists, immigrants, refugees, exiles and so on, each with their own variously changing scripts and behaviour patterns. He does not deny the existence of what he calls the 'warp' of stable communities. But this, he suggests, is shot through with the 'weft' of these other groupings and populations, both intending to move and actually on the move (Appadurai 1996: 33–4). It is useful to consider ethnicity and dress a little in this way with ethnic groups and ethnicity being essentially mobile. Thus the term 'ethnic' clothing becomes im- possible to fix with any degree of certainty, however tempting. It is not exclusively hybrid clothing but attire chosen by the wearer for particular reasons and used in particular ways in different situations. Malaysian women visiting Australia, for instance, may wear their customary dress, that is *baju Malaya*, consisting of *sarong* or *kain*, *kebaya* (long-sleeved upper garment) and head veil.[3] Alternatively they can wear a veil and *kebaya* with jeans and sneakers as a form of holiday wear, or even fully westernised dress, depending on personal choice. Clothes form part of the boundaries that any community, age, or gender related social subset draws around itself. But inevitably these boundaries are defined in fluid relation to those who occupy its borders. Thus 'ethnic' dress must be thought of as relational. It is attire in which the components are never absolutely static or 'frozen', but in continual process. As such, it is dress often strategically assumed, as with the Hmong or Malay women, and of course many others.

Aside from these examples of cultural brokering, many postcolonial indigenous cultures are looking back to the past, re-establishing links with their 'ethnic' origins and dress traditions. Having embraced the attire of the developed world initially, they are endeavouring to re-establish connections to their past for a range of different reasons. It may be a nationalist strategy to recoup a lost past, a reassertion of traditional ideas about gender, a tourist marketing exercise, a reinvention of 'ethnic' identities, or as part of broader cultural, political and economic struggles with western materialism. Indeed some Muslim cultures, notably Iran, have set themselves against western dress practices in favour of their own attire. They have rejected in part, or entirely, the Americanisation of dress, especially for women. In some Islamic cultures even the veil can act as a symbolic form, used to resolve conflicting demands. It can be an 'ethnic' protest at western influences, a sign of religious modesty and at the same time a revitalisation of old ideas about femininity, making them seem appropriate for the modern world (Craik 1994: 29). The maintenance of veil wearing by Muslims can be an even greater imperative when travelling in non-Islamic cultures.

In looking for the various stakeholders in places like the US, the UK, Europe, Australia and Canada who use 'ethnic' elements of dress, one can note the changing temporary fads of urban youth subcultures which draw on aspects of this kind. Michael Maffesoli, Ted Polhemus and others have both used the expression 'style tribalism' to explain the group aesthetics of subculture dress, a metaphor which is by no means universally accepted. Caroline Evans is one historian who has drawn critical attention to this particular terminology which she regards as inappropriate for any post-industrial society, as she feels the term is too close to the notion of 'primitive' social organisation (Evans 1997: 186). In his discussion of youth cultures and the style politics of the street, Ross shows these subcultures with group affiliations may not necessarily be related in any ethnic sense, or have any binding agenda, although they may of course be African American, West Indian, Latino or Muslim. They express them-selves beyond their ethnicity as temporary, loosely cohesive groups, in terms of particular hairstyles or hair sculpture, logos or cheap brand alternatives, sneakers and caps. This may include bootleg gear or parodies of middle of the road clothing and gym body culture. Differing from Evans in that he accepts the term 'tribalism', he calls these cohesive practices a celebration of local style, one where 'everyone cannot be anyone' (Ross 1994: 289).[4] So, as Craik has rightly suggested, western and non-western dress should not necessarily be regarded as diametrically opposed. Rather, all over the world elements from traditional or 'ethnic' dress codes are constantly being played off strategically against western attire, as part of a process of reworking and reformulating new forms of clothing and identities (Craik 1994: 30).

Part of the powerful attraction that the clothes of ethnic others have for European consumers is that they are exotic or seem luxurious or sensuous. They can also be desirable because they signal the handmade, or appear to represent evidence of a simpler way of life. There is of course a very strong attraction for western goods amongst those in the less developed world, as well as a desire for the ethnically foreign (the Muria are a good example). But there are interesting complications associated with longings for the dress of other cultures. The down market Kinshasha *Sapeurs* in Zaire (see chapter 1), developed in a culture that officially promoted ethnicity and discouraged western materialism, seeking wherever possible to acquire the opposite of local dress, that is foreign designer labels. They paraded these foreign status goods as booty, but without the wealth to go with them, in what amounted to a ritual replication, perhaps even an initiation rite (Ross 1994: 286).

This is not just consuming luxury goods as the opposite of necessities. In terms of what Appadurai calls the 'special register' of luxury consumption (Appadurai 1986: 38), *Sapeurs* used luxury items as a rhetorical strategy to register 'difference' from the rest of their society. This is a difference at some distance from status tied to wealth in the western sense. These garments were, if we use Appadurai's terms, 'metonymic' of a larger system of power and prosperity to which, we might suggest, *Sapeurs* sought to pay allegiance (Appadurai 1986: 52). In other countries we find interesting similarities in the lure of foreign 'difference'. Monga, in an account of African women in Douala, the economic capital of Cameroon, argues that certain brand name American garments like T-shirts, and beauty products, especially lipstick, exude a special prestige. In a country whose political and economic future is uncertain, women believe these commodities are not just the latest fashion. Rather to acquire them, in whatever way they can, much like a cargo cult syndrome, confers on the purchaser symbolic status and shows they have the capability to expand their horizons beyond a deprived present. They allow the wearer to participate symbolically in the social modality of the global arena (Monga 2000: 201–2, Appadurai 1986: 52).

Clearly there is some irony in a supposedly homogenised global economy that still places value quite differently on both 'local' and 'foreign' goods. For those in the developed world at least, the lure of 'ethnic' commodities, seems to hinge on an aura of a 'simpler' way of life, utopian visions of peasant life, and nostalgia for the perceived luxury of the handmade, something admired many years before by William Morris. For a world that is more and more industrialised, the supposedly hand-crafted or individually made commodity embodies attractive, unsullied qualities often regarded as characteristic of 'genuine' or 'ethnic' garments, particular to a named location. Yet even these can be marketed worldwide. The broad-brimmed hat, with 'ethnic' patterns in brown, worn by a guide at Lake Titicaca (see Figure 19 in chapter 5), is exactly the same kind of hat widely available at weekend markets in Australia. Equally there are consumers who value 'ethnic' rarity and exclusivity of a more up-market kind. In the case of 'foreign' or exotic goods it can be simply a desire to show evidence of possessing the different, the special or the unusual.

Ethnicity and modernity

Unquestionably the uptake of western dress among non-European cultures, with their own dress traditions, has been both selective and inconsistent.

In some places, thoroughgoing adoption of European dress has taken place only since about the 1970s. In China for example, *shizhuang* or fashion, as a sign of growing links to the international world, emerged only in the mid-1980s (Li 1998: 74–5). Western clothing continues to be combined in some places with traditional dress, or partially adopted with respect to gender and age, or for particular occasions. In many cultures, or subgroups, global clothing is regarded as a sign of progress, as opposed to a clinging on to tradition. Whilst its attraction has been considerable, consumer preferences can sometimes be formally countered by nationalist desires to reinvent traditional dress, or by a self-conscious, often deliberate choice to retain ethnic attire. In nationalist Zaire, under the rule of Mobuto Sese Seko, an 'authenticity' code was enforced that prevented men from wearing coats and ties, and women from wearing jeans. Although not based on national traditions, men in Zaire were required to wear a version of the Mao suit called *abaco* with a cravat and not a tie to express national identity (Biaya 1998: 85). In 1997 President Laurent Kabila, on coming to power in the new Democratic Republic of Congo, put similar prohibitions in place (Hansen 1999: 6).

The uptake of western clothing in the less developed world has varied most obviously according to gender, although in places like Mauritania it may be only children who wear western style attire (Figure 16). Even so, whilst women have been on the whole slower to modernise, they are now widely accepting western dress all over the world, either partially or in its

16 Men and women walking in the oasis town of Chinghuetti, Mauritania 2003. They are mostly dressed in Arab influenced customary attire, with the exception of the young boy nearest the spectator who apparently wears secondhand clothing

entirety. In her account of Indian dress, published in the mid-1990s, Tarlo found married women, other than a small, educated urban elite, continued to wear Indian dress, where men did not (Tarlo 1996: 153). This having been said, fashionable urban women might carry a mixture of clothes in their wardrobe, from the classical Indian sari, to hybrid clothes like the *shalwar kamiza* (tunic and trousers), and chic western clothes and leisure-wear like jeans (Tarlo 1996: 335). Even Indian village women, like the *Bharwads* (pastoral people), are slowly modernising, still dressing in traditional clothing of *kapdu* (upper garment) and *jimi* (waist cloth), but made in cheaper and thinner artificial fabrics such as machine woven polyester (Tarlo 1996: 267). So the penetration of western style clothing is evident if only in part, and, as has been shown, traditional dress itself undergoes modifications and changes of fashion. Interestingly the fascination for western dress can sometimes be less an emulation of the values of the US, than a deliberate decision made by consumers for culturally specific and internal reasons. Research among Bedouin women in Egypt's Western Desert shows they continue to wear traditional dress. Yet they express resistance to the older generation and the power structure of their own culture, by a subtle westernising of veil fabrics and the use of cosmetics (Abu-Lughod 1990: 49–50).

In all cultures, wearing dress that is not your own is undertaken for specific reasons and occasions, and at times can be assumed almost like a provisional or performance costume. Young village men in Egypt who travel to Cairo, for instance, sometimes take on informal western dress. They also have their hair cut short, in order to feel greater security and to pass in the city as someone connected to the power structure of the state (Fandy 1998: 9). This is not upward mobility as such, but a calculated decision to take on the dress of another culture and class for a certain period of time, and thus partake of the benefits of that class. In Mexico, villagers take on a *mestizo* appearance when visiting towns and large markets. But according to Sayer, writing in the 1980s, traditional dress of Mazahua communities could merely be covered over on such trips. In an interesting assumption of bicultural identity or provisional identity, western trousers were worn over *calzones* (drawers) and store bought shirts over customary embroidered ones (Sayer 1985: 229). Yet, as we have seen in Mauritania (see Figure 7 in chapter 1) the reverse can happen, with store bought clothing worn beneath customary attire. There are other examples of bicultural dressing. Tarlo cites a case of a *Rabari* student who changed each day into college clothes of shirt and trousers at a friend's house, returning in the evening to change back into *deshi* (indigenous dress) for the sake of his wife who despised him in European style clothes (Tarlo 1996: 258).

In the Arab world and within the Arab diaspora since the 1970s, attitudes toward western dress have varied widely. Many women have signalled resistance to western dress and materialism by adopting modern versions of traditional headscarves, or in some instances the full *hijab*. Yet in Saudi Arabia there is a quite different response. There ethnicity in dress has become less and less evident. Elite women pride themselves on acquiring luxurious and specially designed Gulf style couture clothing and jewellery as a particular way of signalling status (Yamani 1997: 56 and 60–1). So when educated and cosmopolitan women wear European rather than indigenous dress, it is not everyday clothing. In Egypt, for instance, this attire is western dress at its most expensive and luxurious. This means a woman is willing to go to some considerable expense, and social discomfort, to avoid using the *hijab*, thereby deliberately aligning herself with a wealthy European class, rather than local indigenous culture (Fandy 1998: 7). The wearing of Muslim dress is patently selective and case specific. In Egypt educated working women often wear a hybrid mix of long European style maxi skirt with *hijab*, or a modest head covering, a *mu'adabah*, a cosmopolitan version of the headscarf (Fandy 1998: 7). A further complication arises because the same woman is likely to wear completely customary clothing in her own neighbourhood or after hours. In Bouake, West Africa, women of the professional, urban elite wear mixtures of a tailored *boubous*, that is a half-length or full gown of Islamic origin, or a *complet trois pagnes* with high heel shoes and matching handbag.[5] In addition Muslim women will add a headscarf to either outfit (LeBlanc 2000: 453–4 and 458).

So the relationship between modern dress and customary or 'ethnic' clothing is an intricate weave of habit, defiance, social pressure and taboos, political entanglements and posturing, perhaps too intricate to ever untie completely. Superficially, the ostensibly uniform-like nature, and almost insidious attraction, of some global attire seems to draw nations together at the level of style. Yet it can often be the perception of 'sameness', rather than its actual consumption, that springs to mind in any assessment of worldwide dress. The belief in global uniformity is an exaggeration, obscuring the subtle instances of regional, caste and ethnic differences. Added to this, 'ethnic' dress of all types and varieties is worn alongside global clothing, sometimes even biculturally. Nepal is an interesting example of these complexities. As in other places, such as Eastern Indonesia, the kind of dress one wears is an important way to signal one's state of 'development' and progressiveness, or alternatively one's 'old fashioned' ways. In Nepal, women, like men, are increasingly wearing European dress, but there are still groups of women, identifying themselves with high caste Hindus, who deliberately continue to wear saris. Hindu culture believes itself to be

superior to others and officially encourages sari wearing to indicate association with their 'developed' culture, in this case development is associated
with traditional rather than western dress practices. At the same time,
high-caste Hindu women in Nepal see themselves as more advanced than
their counterparts in the North who wear *chubbas* (long cross-over tunics
tied with a thick sash). They regard these people as 'backward' (Hepburn
2000: 285–6). So all patterns of wearing are clearly inflected by minor
local cultural perceptions of difference and evaluation, and these variations
are meaningful to those who have inside knowledge of local dispositions
and customs, where they may not be evident to others.

Fashionably 'ethnic'

Western high fashion has demonstrated for centuries an unceasing appetite
for novel ideas based on the 'primitive' or the exotic. Designers today, like
corporate raiders, source inspiration indiscriminately from distant cultures,
usually with scant regard for original context. 'Ethnic' and 'national' styles,
culled from one's own backyard or further afield, are a seemingly never
diminishing gold mine of resources, a design pool available for all (Maynard
2000b: 21). The term 'ethnic chic' is sometimes used by journalists to
describe the high fashionable habit of outsiders, that is those who adopt
an ethnic 'look' without any concern for the actual dress traditions of a
culture. Often only shorthand signs of Chinoiserie or Indian decoration
are all that is needed to represent an indigenous culture. Particularly
noteworthy is the lack of specificity in the common use of the term 'ethnic'.
It frequently refers superficially to the appearance of dress that is vaguely
village-like or peasant-like, having a rough, handmade, decorative quality.
Aside from this general appropriation of the idea of ethnicity, western
designers also seamlessly incorporate into their fashions actual items of
traditional dress, textiles and accessories like beads, shawls and earrings.
These are displayed almost as collector's items or even as trophies. European
and US fashion designers, as widely different as Gaultier, Ralph Lauren,
Galliano, and Shirin Guild, have been, and still are in their various ways,
fascinated with ethnic or vernacular designs, with their distinctive qualities
and aura of the 'genuine' or handcrafted. African, Indian, Asian, Mexican,
South American, Iran, Central European folk designs have all been fair
game for fashion designers.

   Importantly we seldom hear what indigenous people feel about this
form of appropriation, or about the ways in which 'native' dress, traditionally
part of complex family systems, symbolisms and frameworks, is undermined
by assimilation, commercialisation and fashion treasure hunters. Yet, one
must bear in mind that catwalk interest in indigenous designs can have the

reverse affect, stimulating and renewing interest in traditional textile practices
and body decoration (Gale and Kaur 2002: 101). An interesting case of
exploitation is documented in Guatemala, a country that in its early history
had hundreds of distinctive village costumes. Only vestiges of pre-Columbian
dress were evident by the late twentieth century. In the 1990s Mayan village
women still wore the traditional *huipil* upper garment, wraparound *corte*
skirt and woven belt, although both men and women wore mixtures of
Mayan and western style clothes. Village men sometimes wore hybrid, even
bicultural outfits, consisting of long pants made of woven Mayan fabric
and topped with short overpants derived from ancient times (Brodman
1994: 272–3). Brodman uses changing Mayan dress practices to highlight
the vulnerability of these native peoples, whose ancient traditions are
gradually being undermined by imported interference. She cites a particular
instance of exploitation on the part of the ruling Ladinos, who liked to
bask in the reflected glory of Mayan heritage. At the annual Folklore Festival
in Cobàn, officials organised a parade of exquisite indigenous garments and
textiles to sell to fashion designers' representatives and buyers from around
the world. Beauty contestants in regional costumes, required by law to
attend, were paraded before the largely foreign audience. This was a source
of humiliation for villagers, but of no financial gain to them (Brodman
1994: 278).

The interweavings between modern fashion and traditional dress are
complex. Tarlo discusses some instances in the 1980s when Indian women
chose to wear extravagant versions of Indian clothing as a form of 'ethnic
chic', with little relationship to actual village dress or traditional clothing.
This was part of a new commercialisation of fashion at the time. Tarlo
raises questions about this apparent return to traditional Indianness in
fashion, suggesting it is a form of masquerade or performance of identity,
a tasteful ethnicity rather than sympathy for local village people (Tarlo
1996: 315). This represents an idealised return to a certain aspect of the
past, safeguarding the exclusivity of the wearers, who are, of course, not
peasants. It also speaks to, and on behalf of, an international audience
rather than a local one (Tarlo 1996: 311). It is also a status seeking practice
according to Tarlo, so that the minority Indian elite can differentiate
themselves from the mass of jeans and sari wearing middle classes. Quite
lacking in social commitment they just play at style, stepping into the
village, at the precise time that the majority of villagers are stepping out
(Tarlo 1996: 324). She quotes the case in 1989 of a glamorous Delhi
socialite of mixed background from a wealthy Lahore family who chose
to 'go ethnic' and to wear the clothes of a low caste *Bungri* woman, while
living an otherwise wealthy life.

At exactly this time Indian fashion designers in Britain began to set up highly successful firms, making garments based on traditional patterns and also importing garments designed in India. In fact an explosion of fashion houses started up in response to a growing middle class of educated professional Indian, and indeed British women, interested in designer clothes that reinterpreted traditional dress and celebrated the cultural roots of migrants (Khan 1992: 64). So culturally mobile Indian women as well as western women were able to wear modifications of 'ethnic' Indian dress produced by Indian designers. Khan argues that this was a practice that suited dual cultural systems, obviating the necessity for choice between east and west, suggesting there was, in the early 1990s, still no uniquely British-Asian fashion (Khan 1992: 70–1). This acceptance of dual fashion systems may appear to be a form of hedging one's bets, yet the political reality is that choice is usually only available to the well-to-do. The fact that no fully hybrid style had emerged by that time means the various circumstances and cultural rationale for choice of wear was different in each case. Clearly 'ethnic' dress has different resonances for different classes and also for Indian women in both India and Britain, compared to British women.

As part of the kind of cultural exchange identified above, the saree, a garment with a very ancient tradition and still worn by older Indian women, has been given a new lease of life in versions made of modern fabrics and colours. Sarees are made in every quality, from the everyday purchase at a sidewalk stall in London suburbs like Alperton or Southall, to more highly exclusive shops selling exquisite designer sarees. Older style sarees are also remodelled into new retro items for sale in places like Camden market (Puwar 2002: 71). The 'new' saree is sold as a fashion and promoted as an advantage for a modern Indian woman, as was western dress previously. As Nag shows in her study of modern Bengali sarees, by the 1990s women were being enticed to buy the 'new' saree by advertising copy that paradoxically did so by using the nostalgic imagery of its past and traditional notions of femininity (Nag 1991: 95). But it is not just the case of redefining the saree, western markets are saturated with unspecific Indian style garments and accessories (Puwar 2002: 67). Fashion designers continually experiment with new versions of the *shalwar* suit, a set of garments made up of trousers, tunic-like *kameez* and co-ordinated *dupatta* or stole. They are also fascinated with the richness of regional Indian dress, incorporating elements from Bhopali *kurtas* and Alighari *pyjamas* into new and partially modern styles (Khan 1992: 64).

The interweaving between traditional Indian dress and European fashion is matched by similar interchanges between Japanese and Chinese dress. Overwhelmingly westernised centres like Hong Kong are returning to their past by inventing modern high fashions and accessories that draw heavily on traditional garments, the *ma kwa* jacket and the *cheung sam* for instance. Interestingly in Hong Kong, especially around the takeover of sovereignty in 1997, the popularity of the latter two garments, revived as modern outfits in polyester not silk, sat well with an expanding conscious-ness of cultural identity (Clark 2000: 03). These garments were also worn in New York by non-Chinese people, sometimes with backpacks and athletic shoes (Clark 1999: 164). This image of Charmaine Leung in 1997 shows her wearing a ready to wear *cheung sam* purchased from 'China Products' department store in Hong Kong (Figure 17). Interestingly she has combined it with casual shoes and shoulder bag, both widely worn global fashions.

Western designers have had a longstanding attraction to Japanese clothing and fabric designs. Traditional kimonos seem to embody sup-posedly timeless qualities, and have been drawn to the bodily design

17 Charmaine Leung wears a readymade cheung sam, with western style sneakers and carry bag, Hong Kong, 1997

aesthetic they express. The Japanese themselves regard traditional kimonos, chiefly used on ceremonial occasions in modern times, as the most beautiful native dress in the world. Its fabrics express the Japanese aesthetic sensibility to the seasons and 'in its folds is layered the soul of Japan' (Dalby 1993: 1). So in different ways, both cultures see symbolic and artistic qualities in the kimono, and for some it almost holds quasi-spiritual qualities. Japanese fashion designers like Issey Miyake and Rei Kawakubo since the 1970s have inspired Europe by producing garments that echoed their own national dress traditions. But interestingly, matching western fascination with Japanese 'ethnicity', the Japanese have redefined the parameters of European haute couture by a turning back to their own native traditions and philosophies, although both Kawakubo and Yamamoto resist the label 'Japanese' (Maynard 2000b: 21).

In an ironic twist, Japanese consumers, drawn in their thousands to tourist venues in Australia, are deeply attracted to the products of cheerful Australian leisurewear designers like Ken Done, Mambo and Balarinji. Of these, Balarinji is the label that most readily complies with an Australian ethnicity, in that it trades on links with indigenous culture, making much of its collaborations between Australian and Aboriginal designers. Balarinji is more than a very successful tourist market provider. In 1992, with acute marketing perception, the company signed an agreement with the Japanese company, Nitto Boseki, to put their designs onto Japanese clothing and accessories. What is interesting is that they specifically rework their Aboriginal type colours in a brighter range for Japanese tastes (Maynard 2001: 176). So, for the Japanese tourist in Australia, and those who shop at boutiques in Tokyo, brightly coloured and breezy Australian clothing signals a type of exotic colourfulness. This paradoxically represents a sort of reverse aesthetic to the traditions of subtlety in Asian design (Owens 1993: 9).

Tourist ethnicity

Global tourism is partly the worldwide search for 'authentic' experiences, that are deemed to be different from the tourist's own culture. Tourist industries all over the world are in the business of vigorously marketing ethnic style or traditional garments, jewellery and fabrics for visitors. These can be anything from Hawaiian shirts to Indonesian sarongs. Garments are claimed as 'authentic' indigenous products, but the labels and markers of this supposed ethnicity are not straightforward reflections of an existing social reality. Producers consciously fabricate these clothes, making them deliberately attractive to souvenir hunters. Certain cultures also increasingly consume their own ethnicity in tourist-like forms, such as Hawaiian T-shirts with ethnic logos sold primarily to locals (Wood 1998: 231). The question is should we call these products 'ethnic' dress? In the act of materially externalising what constitutes ethnicity, tourist souvenirs mark a choice about what constitutes the visible signs of it (Wood 1998: 225). So the answer is that it is only the value placed on such garments, mainly by tourists, that makes them genuinely 'ethnic'.

Eller argues, in a lengthy examination of ethnicity and culture, that whilst ethnicity shares certain cultural markers, it is an elusive, expansive concept about which, there is nothing fixed or immobile (Eller 1997: 554). Ethnicity is a construct, not in some form of continuity with tradition but rather part of a self-consciously remembered past, designed specifically to suit the present. In Eller's view, within nation-building, and one could add, within the sustaining of national identity, 'traditional' or 'authentic' practices are not just statements about ethnic origins. They are likely to be deliberate 'political revernacularisations' of the national or indigenous past, a strategy to make the past palatable and consumable by the present (Eller 1997: 573–4). Ethnic tourism is a way of marketing acceptable forms of traditional commodity, but with a new cast appropriate for modern consumers. This preserves the credible illusion of 'authenticity' whilst at the same time presenting buyers with commodities that suit their contemporary tastes (Hiwasaki 2000: 396).

The production of ethnic tourist products has some clear benefits for local people, as it can help to preserve a culture, its design practices and its identity. Many governments encourage the making of indigenous or 'ethnic' style dress and textile products, perhaps to encourage self-sufficiency amongst indigenous peoples and to provide sources of revenue. In Australia, since the 1970s, T-shirts and sarongs made by Aborigines using textiles printed with customary patterns, have been popular with tourists. These were originally made in community art centres throughout the remote regions of Australia, and some communities continue to engage with this practice. Even so, despite the fact that indigenous people do wear these patterned T-shirts, they are in no way a customary form of dress.

Hepburn, in her study of Thamel cloth clothing, sold in the tourist area of Kathmandu, Nepal, makes some extremely interesting comments about tourist consumption and the ways in which the meanings of clothes made of this fabric shift as they are worn by different groups of people. She notes marked differences between the perceptions of what these clothes signify for tourists and for others. The actual circumstances of their making are worth noting, for Thamel cloth is not indigenous, actually woven in India and imported into Nepal. There it is made into a variety of garments only tokenly like Nepalese clothing (Hepburn 2000: 284). Some tourists buy it, believing it to be genuinely local, piecing it together with other bits of ethnic clothing picked up from Indonesia and India. Others feel that they are helping Tibetan refugees or that the clothing is somehow linked to Tibetan culture. The linking of Thamel cloth with Tibetan refugees, says Hepburn, persists across the Pacific, where students in North America wear it also for altruistic reasons (Hepburn 2000: 292). Of great interest is, that since the mid-1990s, young Nepali men themselves have also started to wear Thamel cloth clothing, in particular an *eystercoat*, or vest, and the *topi* hat, which rests high on the crown with a low peak. Apparently they wear these clothes because what tourists see as Nepali or Tibetan, they see as European, and thus a way of projecting the image of themselves as modern (Hepburn 2000: 294).

Much of the significance of what is labelled 'ethnic' dress by the west lies in the ways different stakeholders variously use and evaluate traditional or indigenous commodities. What we term 'ethnicity' in dress is clearly mutable. At any one time, clothing, hairstyles and body modifications, derived initially from non-western cultures, mean certain things in terms of high fashion in the developed world, but something very different within popular culture, and to those who practice 'alternative' lifestyles. Cosmetic or body arts like Indian and African henna skin painting (*mehndi*) can simultaneously be a symbolic indigenous practice, a European fashion statement (especially popular around 1996), a mass marketed product (2000) but also an 'alternative' lifestyle accessory.[6] Unquestionably customary 'ethnicity', expressed in dress, has been compromised and decontextualised by contact with the west, although the reverse may also be true, and global dress itself is subject to a high degree of variability. But within new configurations that combine both tradition and modernity, clothing reveals that its design is constantly in a state of flux, and that it continues to convey important and differentially decoded messages about change within the global environment.

Notes

1 *Molas* are symbolic designs made from applied layers of cloth that are cut away in decorative shapes to reveal contrasting colours.

2 The 'global ecumene' is a phrase sometimes used in place of globalisation (Wassmann 1998: 3).

3 A *kain* is a wrapping cloth or skirt, while a *sarong* is a tube made of two strips of cloth sewn together.

4 Daniel Rosenblatt in his account of what he terms 'modern primitive' dress in the US, discusses tattooing as a 'tribal marker'. He argues that modern tattooing is both a public and a private act – that it is intended as a way of identifying with others in a group, but overwhelmingly an expression of self-identity (Rosenblatt 1997: 306–7).

5 A *pagne* refers to a wrapped item of clothing, a factory printed textile or a two-metre length of cloth.

6 Henna body painting started to became very popular in the west in the mid-1990s. There is some suggestion that it was regarded as a timeless practice and a safe alternative to tattooing. It marks a western fascination with things Indian at the time, including film and literature, as well as a way of demonstrating a form of unproblematic multiculturalism (Hassan 1998: 122).

5 ✧ Style and communication

Daddy – Why is that Man Wearing a Blank T-shirt? (*Reader's Digest Cartoon* 1998)

ALL CLOTHING is a form of communication, as the mutable factors of ethnicity in dress clearly exemplify. Over the years cultural theorists and historians have attempted to explain the complicated ways in which information about class, gender, race and occupation is exchanged through the medium of attire. If any understanding of the subtleties and uneven articulations between universal, local (or personal) meanings in global dress is to be achieved, the issue of communication must be addressed. Undertaking pioneering work in seminology, the structuralist Roland Barthes used theories of language to analyse various cultural signifying systems, the most relevant for dress studies being his famous text *The Fashion System* (1983). Working primarily with fashion photographs and the way they communicate, rather than actual clothing, he broke down the structural aspects of dress into the conceptual opposition between written clothing and imaged clothing. He proposed that dress, especially represented dress, is made up of changing and paradoxical relations between the social institutional aspects of style, those that conform to language, and individualised, actualised dress as worn being the equivalent of speech (Barthes 1983: 17–18). His objective was not to address clothing or language per se, but the translation of the one into the other. More recently, and more literal in approach, is the work of Alison Lurie who claims clothes are almost the equivalent of words and sentences. She suggests there are many different languages of attire, each with its own grammar and vocabulary, whose meanings can be read almost as if one were looking at a book (Lurie 1992: 4). She says that 'We put on clothing for some of the same reasons that we speak: to make living and working easier and more comfortable, to proclaim (or disguise) our identities and attract erotic attention' (Lurie 1992: 7). She even suggests there are sartorial equivalents of foreign languages and accents (Lurie 1992: 84).

Given what we know about identity as provisional, Lurie's approach would seem to be a method of explanation rather too uncomplicated and mechanistic, although there are clearly many ways in which dress and language have elements in common. National dress and language is one good example. Borrowings across languages, as in creole or pidgin, can also transform and reshape cultural identity, making interesting parallels with hybrid dress forms that mix local and 'foreign' elements (Lindisfarne-Tapper and Ingham 1997: 4). But to concentrate on itemising elements in a language of dress or fashion is to be overly prescriptive, and assumes that wearer and decoder have common cultural understandings. Anne Hollander, best known for her theory that fashion is a self-perpetuating visual fiction, is adamant that clothes should not be compared to statements or verbal behaviour (Hollander 1980: xv). She maintains inward convictions about one's dress are often different from specific meaningfulness – 'out in public space nobody has to be responsible for rightly perceiving the modes he does not know or care about, but everybody nevertheless responds to what he sees … the famous messages allegedly sent by clothes are not always the same ones as those received …' (Hollander 1993: 123–4). Indeed in our fragmented, postindustrial world, there is more likely to be an aggregation of disparate dress codes, even dialects, which are not commonly understood (Crane 2000: 247). So to suggest that clothing is a language is to leave unacknowledged its complex and variable contexts of wearing, and may ignore the fact that communication can be as subtle even as embodied practice and sensibility (Durham 1999: 391).

For some time the whole idea that dress is a straightforward conveyor of information, either verbal or non-verbal, has been under review by dress historians, cultural theorists and anthropologists.[1] Fred Davis has pointed to the limitations of conflating clothes unproblematically with language, suggesting that clothing is undercoded in comparison to written language, and that its meanings are imprecise, ambiguous and often quite unreliable (Davis 1992: 5). It has even been suggested that there are few grounds for claiming clothing constitutes a language at all, especially as there are no rules or formulae that govern the practice (Campbell 1997: 346). Whatever the case, most commentators now agree that all forms of clothing are culturally relative; their meanings alter over time and can be differentially interpreted especially across cultures. Global media networks have contributed to the spread of style, adding even further complications to the decoding of messages. Even those who do accept dress to be a non-verbal mode of communication, need to accept that social groupings are no longer categoric or fully exclusionary, and as a result we must acknowledge that there are many different, often ambiguous, modalities through which dress meanings are constituted.

If clothes are not precisely readable, how can we assess them? Barnard for one has recently undertaken a close analysis of the cultural production and exchange of meanings, in a study of the connections between fashion and communication. Addressing himself to western dress practices, he argues that fashion, and other clothing, does not generate meaning in any obvious manner but communicates in more complex and relational ways than straightforward language. He also sees dress specifically, and in a challenging sense, as embedded in ideological struggles to achieve power and status. Speaking of a battle against hegemony, he uses the metaphor of 'weapons' and 'defences' as a way of understanding the clothing tactics of subordinate social groups, whether of class, race or gender. These different ways of wearing may sustain hierarchical position, achieve group cohesion within any given social order but can also at times be used to challenge it (Barnard 1996: 38–9).

One of the major problems with Barnard's metaphor is that it fails to take account of dress that deliberately or inadvertently confuses meaning. Missing the subtle tactics and nuances of clothing, his text assumes a slightly aggressive stance. It suits the interpretation of resistant strategies in early western subculture dressing but even here there are problems. Caroline Evans has argued in her important analysis of 1980s and 1990s subcultural activities, that we need to rethink the nature of, and also our understanding of, the dressed identities of such groups. The rationale for her revision is a claim that past accounts of subcultures have tended to fix identities rather than recognise their more likely fluid and unstable nature. At the same time mainstream society itself, has become less coherent (Evans 1997: 170). In a very useful way Evans sees more complexity in dress than the former sharp binaries of dominant versus resistant, implicit in standard writings on the subject including that of Barnard. As part of what she terms 'repertoires of resistance' she asks for a new, more problematic model of subculture, and indeed a new model of culture, that is more heterogeneous, one that accounts for global as well as local differences. She shows that resistance in subcultures is never static, as these groupings move or process through various changing identifications and affiliations (Evans 1997: 183). Resistance can also be encompassed by passive understatements. Evans offers as an example the fairly bland style of late 1980s ravers who deliberately chose dress that was anonymous. This blandness, verging on invisibility, made it resistant to mainstream culture thus unable to be co-opted by the market as punk had been (Evans 1997: 178). Dress then can be quite obtuse. It can offer instances of far less ideologically robust forms of meaningfulness than Barnard would have us believe. It also is a practice than can have significance through its material tactility and aesthetics. Individuals, if they have the means, make personal choices about their dress and so clothes are not necessarily adamant, but able to imply identity or signal temporary affiliations with considerable subtlety.

The circumstances of using secondhand clothes, or *salaula*, can be used as a telling example of the complexity of meanings in a global context. In Zambia, many wear a recognisable global kind of attire; for men, suits and ties, and for women, skirts and loose blouses or dresses, sometimes with a wrapper called a *chitenge* (Hansen 2000: 259). But the important aspect of these clothes is that they are both secondhand, worn by the less privileged, but also part of 'cutting a good figure in Zambian terms'. The casual western observer may see *salaula* simply as cast off clothing but to a local viewer they have nuanced meanings that relate to being 'well-turned out'. So whilst the reason for third world poverty is a matter of global political dynamics, this clothing cannot be regarded as precisely ideological in Barnard's terms. The act of choosing items involves much work, directed to achieving a unique 'look', one that is bright and neat, delineated in terms of global fashion but with room for local idiosyncrasies and the incongruous (Hansen 2000: 257). We must attach a similar degree of importance to local interpretations of clothes worn in Egypt. For example, oasis and village dwellers have increasing access to urban style goods, and young women wearing western dresses are found all over the country. This has infringed upon customary dress, most often worn by married women, consisting of a mixture of long print gowns and black head shawls (Figure 18). Village women who visit Cairo prefer urban-influenced clothes in floral designs, with cuffs, collars and buttons, rather than such loose robes. Observers know that cut and sewn garments are more expensive than traditional garments. So urban-influenced clothes, termed 'short foreign style dresses', inform those who understand that the wearer has greater sophistication than a rural villager (Spring and Hudson 1995: 92). There is little doubt that those who choose clothing such as this, do so to fulfil their own precise social intentions. Yet such messages are not necessarily so precisely decoded. They might well be overlooked by an outsider, or someone unfamiliar with local repertoires of dress signals.

In fact social communication can occasionally be as frustrated by clothes as facilitated by them. If we subscribe to the notion of an increasing sameness or Americanisation in global clothing, we might assume the reading of dress to be straightforward. But it is the proposition of this book that there are uneven, and complicated entanglements in clothing that occur between the general 'sameness' of western dress and more localised patterns of wearing. Nor can we assume customary understandings

18 Women, predominantly in customary print gowns and black head shawls, shopping at a Luxor stall, 1990–91

of dress are in any way understood universally. Fieldwork amongst the Herero, undertaken in Botswana by Durham in the late 1980s and early 1990s, produced evidence of what she calls an unstable, 'slippery over-abundance of meaning' bound up in their dress (Durham 1999: 391). She found there to be a marked inversion of common western assumptions about the dynamic between 'traditional' attire and the encroachment of imported dress. The Herero actually regard their own attire as much transnational as ethnic. Herero women and girls also accepted that blouses, skirts and dresses were western styles but did not associate them particularly with Europe or America, places irrelevant to their aspirations. In fact few people had the financial means to be able to buy into fashionable changes. Instead they carefully distinguished southern African dress and that seen as being European, African American and west African (Durham 1999: 400–1). Interestingly the wearing of customary Herero dress signalled a sense of choice and personal agency, whereas passivity and lack of choice was deemed characteristic of those wearing contemporary local, or modern dress. As well as aesthetic style, women in Herero dress were also under-stood and appreciated in ways that included personal embodiment, that is in terms of the ways they moved in this kind of clothing, and its degree of weight and mass (Durham 1999: 392–3).

Westerners need to avoid misunderstanding dress signals of the under developed world. One of the interesting issues in relation to sold-on dress is the relationship to western branding. Unlike new western products, secondhand clothes with imprint logos have no intrinsic or direct meaningfulness that can be linked to the economic status of the wearer, even though the trademark may well have been chosen with care. Appadurai and Mathews support this evident complication when they question the US as a disseminator of brands, values and therefore a controller of meanings. But even so the tenaciousness of the brand or logo is such that it survives the fact of being sold-on. It thus retains some of its significance, although prestige still resides in the capacity to purchase new branded clothing rather than sold-on goods. So, there are clear discrepancies between branded meanings, as generated by vast global companies, and the day to day purchasing of brands in local, perhaps non-metropolitan markets. More interestingly, Hansen found that young men in Zambia were more interested in the 'big look', that is the fashionable cut of branded secondhand clothes than the fashionable brand names themselves (Hansen 2000: 269).

The fact that customers like these have individual preferences and requirements outside the force of branded goods, some of which relate to their economic status or their ethnicity, means that we need to jettison any belief in universal forms of consumption or notions of uniform meanings. In customary societies one was likely to know the standing and possibly the derivation of someone from their dress, and thus how to assess and to respond to them. But liberalism, and western preoccupation with individualism, has encouraged the importance of creating one's own identity and appearance. Interestingly, when researcher Lynch studied Laotian refugee Hmong people living in the US in 1989, she found complications had arisen in respect of dress and identity. Teenagers chose to share a common Laotian ethnicity in dress which was made of American fabric for special occasions, a style Lynch terms 'American Hmong'. This constructed American ethnic identity was quite different from the dress originally worn by the many Hmong subgroups in their country of birth. The reason refugees gave for changing to a common ethnic identity was that in Laos people 'wear what you are', but in America you wear 'the style' that you like. Thus Hmong youth chose variously to conform to US practice by wearing American style dress for some activities but alternatively 'American Hmong' for special celebrations (Lynch 1995: 258 and 262). The original and multifarious styles of their country of origin were never worn.

In the developed world we shape our identity and choice of clothing by comparing our appearances to others in our own social sphere, but we also define ourselves in relation to the wider market. What is fascinating is that this also seems to be the way *salaula* consumption works in Zambia, and indeed has similarities to dress practices among the Herero in Botswana. Western clothing consumers, be they an elite market segment or more middle of the road, are increasingly offered a range of cultural choices, or the illusion of free choice, although even this is likely to be a menu of items, not an unlimited selection (Miles 1998: 105). What is on offer can be a worldwide brand or else directed toward the more personal or cultural sensitivities of consumers. Local tastes and preferences are evidently being consciously mapped onto the universal branded product.[2] For instance, whilst a clothing company like Nike promotes the notion of enfolding all within their universal brand consciousness, there are global clothing firms, Paul Smith for example, that deliberately cater to more local requirements. Paul Smith (with shops all over the world) has interestingly become the number one selling brand in Japan. This, it seems, is partly due to the firm's canny marketing of traditional and street style Britishness, but especially a meticulous attention to local Japanese customs and culture (Crewe and Goodrum 2000: 43). So even the big brands are now coming to recognise the subtle proclivities of local forms of consumption.

Identity versus branding

Equating dress too simplistically with someone's identity is a vexed issue in our global society, in particular one which places such emphasis on the commercial benefits of worldwide consumption. Where can we possibly find common ground between the global branded product and the signalling of personal identity? In the developed world we are proud of our individuality and our capacity to choose who we are, even despite the force and restrictions exerted by branded goods. For the most part we have the economic wealth to freely and individually perform our identities should we so wish, constrained only by officialdom. Even so, we face an institutional environment that is not so flexible or so forgiving, one more and more demanding of pin numbers and identity cards, to prove that we are who we claim. Set against all these issues are the diasporic shifts of communities and movements of populations that might give the impression that emphatic signs of cultural identity in appearance are more mutable. Yet for all cultures appearance remains one of the crucial obsessions of the early twenty-first century. As customary dress is abandoned, subgroups of people all over the world are seeking to reconfirm their ethnicity through clothing, albeit it sometimes a revised set of modalities. This can be achieved by a partial recuperation of customary dress or, in some instances, the abandoning of aspects of those features having lost meaning for the new generation (Seng and Wass 1995: 243).

How then are the tactical meanings of global clothing affected by logos? Superficially brands seem an archetypal example of universal type-casting or easy labelling, and thus of immediate comprehension. Brands urge the fixing of identity and the labelling of taste under the talismanic signs of powerful global corporations like Nike, GAP, Adidas, and even Tommy Hilfiger. The latter is an interesting case where the appeal and meaningfulness of his 'lifestyle' products relate to an especially wide range of consumers. Selling his franchised logo to a fairly affluent international mass, multi-racial youth market, Hilfiger nevertheless has a marketing strategy more akin to old style couture (Taylor 2000: 136). So Hilfiger's logo has a foot in each camp, with a very broad base in the middle market yet catering to celebrities and purveying the aura of exclusivity. But in general, branded clothing marks out the wearer as part of a group of similar consumers, in which personal identity plays little part.

The power of companies selling branded clothing is considerable. Academics and global protesters alike continue to debate their influence and affect. Large corporations, Nike in particular, have been singled out by Naomi Klein in her book *No Logo* (2000) for their imperialistic business tactics, saturation advertising and exploitative production practices in third world countries. Nike was also targeted at world trade talks, protestors claiming that such companies are profiting from global markets while undermining the lives of workers in their under resourced factories. Benetton has been subjected to other kinds of complaint. In January 2000 they ran the damaging 'We On Death Row' advertising campaign that caused Sears Roebuck to withdraw from selling Benetton products in their numerous US stores (Ehrenreich 2000: 20).

Branded garments have a curious position within the global market-place. If we take Nike as an example, their 'Swoosh' logo, strategically placed on the wearer's chest (or elsewhere), persistently draws the eye of the viewer like a magnet. Everyone who wears a Nike shirt effectively acts as a mobile and universal advertisement for the company, including the poor in their secondhand garments. But more significantly, branded garments are lawless, without links to geographical place and local time, and so are truly global. Theorists of global space and time help to explain something of the geographical workings of brands. Virilio offers some insight into the relationship that clothing has with such new spatial dispositions and possibilities in *The Vision Machine* (1994). Speaking about technologies of perception and intense image dissemination, he proposes that we live in the instantaneous ubiquity of a visually over-stimulated social environment. Here time and space have become relative: 'time frequency of light has become a determining factor in the apperception of phenomena, leaving the spatial frequency of matter for dead' (Virilio

1994: 71). What he terms the embedded 'extensive' time of the past, with expectations, potentialities and a clearly laid out future, has now been replaced by harsh 'intensive' time. In his terms, ours is a world that stems from a system of message-intensification and independence of images, which is a world with no context (Virilio 1994: 14). This has certain implications for the study of brands, and, as we will see, for T-shirts. The illusion of durability fostered by the branding of products like Nike, shows the brand as a symbol of cross-national commodification transcending geographical space and time. The 'brand' occupies new uncontextualised territory, erasing our normal historical understandings of nation states, their commerce and their productivity (Lury 1999: 503–8).

Brands mark out a new and global territory spatially but more importantly they mark it out symbolically. Logos constitute what Lury has recently termed 'directional symbols', which disregard former known boundaries of cultural and social space. Branded products are of course physical garments, but they also occupy other illusionary spaces, operating in what she calls 'lost time', outside former historical or geographical understandings of the nation-state. This makes them ubiquitous and it is this very ubiquity that makes them immensely profitable. Their livelihood (production) and liveliness (symbolism), once tied together in a former phase of capitalism, are in effect unconnected, although closely and strategically co-ordinated by the parent company (Lury 1999: 508). The persistent and universal presence of the logo creates a false sense of durability and strength in the mind of the consumer, which of course is merely an illusion.

So brands invite the instant and universal meaningfulness associated with global products and their consumption. Yet, running in tandem with this ostensible and direct meaningfulness, is a more complex form of obfuscation. Assuming that branded clothes communicate directly may be to misunderstand the real affect of their messages. Take for instance the manner in which a brand name can be disseminated via the media. Here it is difficult to assess from whom the information is being sent. Is it the manufacturer, the wearer or the person who talks about it on TV? In the words of Umberto Eco, 'There is no longer Authority all on its own ... All are in it, and all are outside it: power is illusive, and there is no longer any telling where the "plan" comes from, and whose ideology is being produced' (Eco quoted in Bastian 1996: 111). It would seem that there is a sense of confusion implicit in branded clothing, one that seems to offer far less explicit information and direct interpretation than previously assumed.

Here one could cite the fact that in every part of the world, canny manufacturers steal branded logos and produce fake goods for sale at a far lower price than the real thing, further confusing any notion of precise

meaningfulness. As well, many consumers seem to be less and less con-
vinced about the importance of branded products. Style appears increasingly
provisional, even uncommitted. Retro is a case in point. Choice of branded
trainer shoes, for instance, used to be a firm style giveaway. Today many
young people have forsaken their branded trainer for retro sneakers and
'old-skool' trainers. If you have both new tech and old, it's harder to read
who you are from your shoes (Jackson 2001: 20). So whilst on the one
hand branded garments speak of a precise link to a global company, and
appear to be informationally direct, on the other they can be worn without
commitment or even be faked. All of this confuses and complicates our
understanding of clothes as precise vehicles of communication within the
global framework.

T-shirt style

T-shirts, either long or short sleeved, are garments we most obviously
associate with meaningful communication in terms of brands and localised
messages. One could argue that T-shirt wearing is the material equivalent
of something like a personal tattoo. Often considered unworthy of critical
attention, the everyday cultural information provided by T-shirts is an
important factor in understanding the nature of globalisation. Originating
in working and service men's undergarments, T-shirts are on the whole
mundane, quite unobtrusive articles of clothing and amongst the com-
monest of mass-produced garments. Comfortable, genderless and popular,
they are worn by men, women and children of all races and social strata
throughout the world, in cities, suburbs and rural areas. They are sold
everywhere – occasionally in up market designer wear, but more often in
conventional department stores, in kiosks and tourist outlets, and perfectly
suited to mail order selling, e-commerce and community markets.[3] They
can be worn at any time of the day or night, as street wear, under jackets,
as nightwear, tank tops and as leisure wear in gyms, on sports fields or
on the beach. Much the same looking garments, plain, or with generic
imprint logos, are found in stores from Australia, Africa, South America
and Europe, in the USA and in the remote corners of Asia. They may be
blank or single colour garments, and as such almost nondescript. At other
times imprinted messages convey particular ethnic or political viewpoints,
for social pressure groups, subcultures and alternative communities. There
is also the fact that T-shirts can be a particular sign of a disadvantaged
and impoverished existence.

It is useful to consider the everyday wearing of T-shirts in relation to
Bourdieu's notion of the 'habitus', or a cultural and social disposition. He
claims different class groupings have their own embodied 'habitus', or sets

of dispositions produced by social proclivities such as taste, behaviours and speech (Entwistle 2000a: 36). As a theoretical model, the 'habitus' allows us to think further about T-shirts, worn as they are so widely and variously by different classes within global social structures. They can be everyday garments for the so-called under classes, that is part of particular sets of bodily dispositions in Bourdieu's terms. But in other circumstances, and as part of other social contexts, they can be high fashion products with chic designer logos for which affluent consumers pay exorbitant prices. Yet the worn-out, dilapidated T-shirt can be as much a leisure choice for the wealthy, as a necessity for the poor. So while these garments are variously worn across classes, they are not intrinsic to a particular social grouping. There are many different classes of T-shirt, but they can themselves be without absolute links to class.

How then can we determine the nature of meanings in T-shirts? One could argue that T-shirts, with their headline-type capacity to display the topical, exemplify the concept that clothing communicates information quickly and effectively. The simple rectangular cut of the shirt seems an ideal page-like shape on which to display the shifting signs and information of our society. These can be brand names, humour, political persuasion, advertising, commemoration, team loyalty, folkloric signs, patriotism, nationalism and subcultural membership. In this respect T-shirts are often ephemeral garments, engaging with topical ideas, viewpoints and events (Martin and Koda 1992). Sometimes they seem to take part in a popular cultural game, rather like a video game, bumper sticker or a spoken flurry of jokes or deal in subversion, cynicism, even social critique or self-reflexive irony.

As the clothing of the streets, they can demonstrate shifts in meaning even in a matter of weeks. In 1991, according to Martin, New York Levi's T-shirts were emblazoned with 'Button Your Fly' as a promotional gift with the purchase of 'authentic' buttoned jeans. The legitimate T-shirts with copyright logo were immediately copied for street sale at a lesser quality. In spring of that year a third form appeared in the 'rapid succession of street-cued, smart alek fashion' when it was altered to read 'Unbutton My Fly' (Martin 1992: 29). This constituted, in Martin's terms, a form of popular fashion dialogue conducted back and forth on the street. Clothes here act almost like a daily newspaper or broadsheet, where street talk is immediately reflected back into actual consumption.

But there is another side to T-shirts and their logo messages, for they can be a little like the performative dress of subcultures discussed by Evans. They are dissembling garments that have no absolute or fixed position. This makes them less like billboards and more items whose significance lies embedded in a network of meanings. An example of the uncertain messages of logo shirts is well illustrated by a guide on Lake Titicaca, Bolivia, photographed in 1999 (Figure 19). He wears a shirt with a totally incongruous imprint referring to a rural industry in New Hampshire, US, in addition to his other garments of local origin. If we turn to the theoretical writings of Derrida, and his view of the detachable nature of the written sign, we find interesting issues we can use to explain the T-shirt's capacity for indirect communication, and indeed to its lack of precise meaningfulness. In *Signature Event Context* Derrida argues that the written sign does not exhaust itself at the moment of inscription, but that structurally it carries with it a force that allows it to break from its context. It is cut off from its 'production' or origin. Thus no context can enclose it, and the rupture then allows other possibilities to be recognised in it (Derrida 1988: 9–10). What happens if we apply this notion of the force of the sign to the T-shirt? Signification can migrate away from its original context. A message may be intended to arouse a thought, but the thought aroused may be entirely different in context from one person to another, one geographical place to another. Something like 'Life is a contact sport' can have a variety of interpretations depending on the viewer's gender and age. So apart from simple interpretation of epigrams, logo shirts can be enigmatic, and can parody and send erroneous signals, especially when worn out of context or if they are secondhand. And what about those who wear old shirts with messages that are completely out of date or simply without meaning to the wearer or the decoder?

19 A tourist guide wearing a US style sweater, dark glasses, local hat and waistcoat, Lake Titicaca, 1999

Significantly, T-shirts can equally be part of a wordless form of communication through style of wearing only rather than their logos. This has been particularly relevant in signalling solidarity amongst subculture groups. In 2001, young black males at a US housing project in Troy, New York and at Albany were seen wearing two regular shirts, one reasonably tight fitting and the other larger and looser. Usually both, but almost certainly the outer one, was white. This was usually worn inside out, so that the brand or care label was clearly visible, usually large. The outer shirt (sometimes with three-quarter or full-length sleeves) was worn only on one arm and over the head, while the other armhole sat on the shoulder. The right arm was not put into the right sleeve and armhole, giving a bunched up, half-dressed look.[4] While we should not construe dress as language or writing as such, clearly clothes can communicate by the style of wearing just as much as via slogans.

In our branded and generic world we expect T-shirts to be 'readable'. For the 'do it yourself style' or 'shopping for identity' of the twenty-first century, they are perfect products for our demand-led consumer patterns, marked by niche marketing, segmentation and diversification. They are garments of generic style as well as garments of individual choice for consumers who actively seek to construct an appearance. On the other hand, they sometimes are, but often do not yield information as directly as it might seem. How often does one see someone in a T-shirt whose message is irrelevant, absurd, completely out of date or simply inappropriate?[5]

There is no doubt T-shirt style can deceive; it can disavow or convey contradictory, even outmoded information, especially if the original context or pattern of its wearing is lost or passé. As a general rule, we should not regard them as evidential or straightforward. T-shirts are a model for understanding some of the complications of global attire, for they are a basic, all-purpose form of clothing which is universal in application. But the fascinating thing is that T-shirts can equally be garments of infinite diversity and inflection, all of which frustrates easy understanding. They are the garments that best signal the world of 'difference' which our global dressing implies.

Notes

1 See Breward 1998 for an account of the debates in fashion and dress history since the early 1990s.

2 Coca Cola's marketing initiatives in 2001 sought to revise hegemonic marketing instructions from central headquarters, to allow more decisions at the national level, and more freedom to local or domestic managers felt to have sensitivity to local tastes. While not strictly speaking a novel idea, the company catch cry at this point in time, at least, was 'think local and act local' (McIntyre 2001: 9).

3 Many internet sites focus entirely on these garments, like 'The T-Shirt Mall', with its multiple categories of slogans and types, or www.T.Shirts.com, accessed February 2002, where the consumer can design their own shirt from a wide range of motif options.

4 This information was supplied by Sean Rintel, doing ethnographic fieldwork in October 2001. My thanks for this useful observation.

5 Besides carrying inappropriate messages, they can be worn in inappropriate places, such as the UCLA T-shirts James Clifford saw all over the Pacific on one of his trips (Clifford 1992: 114).

6 ✧ Headwear:
negotiating meaning

From the moment he took the podium the audience was galvanised –
at last, England had produced an academic with a decent haircut.
(A description of Dick Hebdige lecturing on *Subculture. The Meaning of
Style* in Sydney, *Australian* 1992)

HEADWEAR, hairstyling and decoration of the head have special
significance to cultures around the globe, for all societies regard
that which grows from, covers or embellishes the head as something meaningful. This is an importance recognised by social and dress
historians, anthropologists, sociologists, ethnologists and students of psy-
chology alike. Of course everyday hairdressing can be unremarkable
practice, as are hats and helmets which can be simply worn for protection.
But there is far more to headwear and hairstyling than this. Headwear can
have a universal global relevance, such as the baseball cap, but can, at the
same time, be a tactical marker of ethnicity, status, social cohesion, political
affiliation, fashionable tastes and ethnic, national or group membership.
For a wide variety of cultural and religious reasons bishops wear mitres,
judges wear wigs, lawn bowlers wear broad brimmed hats, Rastafarians
and snowboarders wear dreadlocks, graduates wear mortar boards, Muslims
wear veils, Buddhists and Hindu penitents shave their heads, and *sadhu*
neglect their hair. But dressing of the head, as a popular practice, can also
reinvigorate, rework, subvert or resist all kinds of clothing categories.
Furthermore hats and hair dressing sometimes take up a place 'in between'
other clothing styles that are precisely delineated, or they assume a form
of challenging hybridity that acknowledges the act of cultural assimilation.
One can say that wear for the head cogently demonstrates the unevenness
of global clothing styles, that fluctuate irregularly between the overarching
and the local.

In western culture, hairstyling is an aspect of human adornment that
taps deep-seated emotions and sensitivities. It is a subjective form of attire,

closely linked to beliefs about the body and the self as defined in relation
to others. For many other cultures though, hair and headwear are more
likely to have meanings linked to ethnicity, age and life stage, than to
personality. Yet we must beware of over determining the meanings of
headwear. It has been shown that young UK Muslim women in the 1990s
took pride in veil wearing but reworked the meanings of Asian dress, not
wanting to submit entirely to the dominant meanings it had in Britain.
Looking at this as an outsider, one might have read the veiling in terms
of its formal cultural usage. Instead, close research of their practices of
dressing showed that these young women sought instead to define their
own identity by a more personal choice of clothes, including veiling (Dwyer
1999: 12).

Whilst hair and headwear can be personal signifiers in some cultures,
they can also be symbolic of wider processes of social identity. Among
the semi-nomadic Moslem Tuareg people of North Eastern Niger, for
instance, the elaborate care and adornment of the head shows it to have
extraordinary metonymic significance within their wider social organisation
(Rasmussen 1991–2: 101).[1] Headdresses, such as headscarves for women
(*afar*), and the men's face veil (*tagelmust*), wrapped like a low turban, are
worn in a subtle variety of ways. These various ways of wearing embody
information about status, prestige, age, respect, rites of passage, ambiguities,
and kinship relating specifically to property access within the Tuareg's
inheritance system. So as an extension of the head and hair, these garments
do far more than establish identity or escape from it. They are a kind of
language register of Tuareg society, expressive of mutual behavioural
expectations (Rasmussen 1991–2: 115). But, as is the case with the Muslim
veil worn in the UK, language registers of dress are inherently unstable.
They may undergo change and accommodation, especially where one
culture intersects with another at the meeting places of gender, class, culture
and race. So we must be careful of prescriptive or stereotypical readings.
A case in point is the headband, an article which can be variously used
as an athlete's sweatband, a fashionable accessory or as a sign of rebellion,
as with red bandannas worn by indigenous activists in Australia, rebel
fighters in Indonesia, or the white 'Gus Dur' headbands signalling support
for former President Abdurrahman Wahid.[2]

Unquestionably dress for the head offers a wide and prolific field of
investigation regarding issues of identity, particularly where individuals and
social groups negotiate their similarities or differences. Whilst acknowledging that this aspect of appearance can be one of the most culturally
sensitive elements of anyone's attire, this chapter considers issues pertinent
to hat wearing and hairstyles specifically in terms of shifting meanings
within global patterns of consumption. The intention is to focus on three

quite particular categories of headwear and hairstyles. Whilst there are many possible instances one could have considered, the examples chosen here signify the complex ways identity formation is an ongoing and continually changing process within the global environment. They cogently demonstrate how cultures continue to invest significantly in the symbolism of hair and headwear. The first example is hairstyling, in particular the 'Afro' and dreadlocks, styles which function variously as part of black politics, as anti-mainstream or alternative lifestyle practices and also as fashionable transcultural commodities. The second is the headscarf worn for a variety of reasons by Muslim women as a cultural and especially religious signifier. The third deals with the intricacies of hat wearing, as signs of ritual, ethnic and nationalist dressing.

Hairstyling

Hairdressing is a cultural practice that is an important public symbol across a wide spectrum of peoples, from South East Asia to Europe, Africa and the Americas. Hiltebeitel argues in 'Hair Tropes', the introductory essay to his co-edited text *Hair: Its Power and Meaning in Asian Cultures*, that in one sense hair seems to be quite 'ordinary stuff'. Yet it is difficult to discern what is ordinary about it. It is also difficult to determine what makes it extraordinary, because of its vast and differing social manifestations. He comes to the view that hair can be used methodologically to explain all kinds of social engagements and that in fact 'it begins to look as if nothing is ordinary about hair' (Hiltebeitel 1998: 2). Hiltebeitel claims the symbolism of hair imposes its own differing forms of grammar, but that like any language this grammar is by no means constant or rigid (much as has been shown for the vernacular of dress). Hairdressing operates within a web of social meanings, both of a ritual kind, as well as those related to everyday use (Hiltebeitel 1998: 13). It carries particular meanings in terms of signalling ethnic bonding, membership of a subgroup, conferring religious status and defining maturity. Hairstyles can also convey meanings that suggest cultural hybridity. This sense of constant change and exchange in hair styling, that takes place when groups or individuals interact with one another, or move from one culture to another, forms the basis of this present discussion. Traditional hair practices, for instance, can come under threat when immigrants begin to integrate in a new culture. In India, women's long braided hair was traditionally a clearly understood code of identity, indicating their marital and moral position in society. Its symbolism was defined but extremely complex (B. D. Miller 1998: 275). In America, migrant Indian women have responded to their new environment in the various ways they dress, one aspect being to modernise and cut their hair shorter. So the oiled braid has been all but abandoned except by older women and the very conservative.

Olivelle, discussing the social significance of hair in Asian cultures, analyses hair practices and meanings under a set of specific headings. These include his view that for men and women in the public eye, controlled, groomed hair (or its enclosure in a turban), or braided or coiled hair for women, indicates those willing to submit to customary society's strictures; loose or long hair is associated with femininity in private or domestic life and can even mean sexual informality; shorn hair is a sign of ritual separation related to initiation or incarceration; and finally neglected hair is associated with withdrawal outside civilised social activities or with the morally loose (Olivelle 1998: 12 and 39–40). Supporting Olivelle is the western tradition that long hair in women is a key attribute of youthful femininity, even virginity. But Olivelle's conclusions about gender are difficult to sustain within a global framework and the findings cannot be simply extrapolated. Sikh men, living in the UK, wear hair long beneath their turbans, so long hair can be a symbol of masculinity as well as femininity. For a whole postwar generation in Western Europe, the US, Australia and white Southern Africa, long hair has been a social indicator of some importance and a practice that engendered anxieties when 'hippies' challenged orthodox social boundaries in the 1960s. Echoes of these fears still remain in respect of 'dreadlocks', tightly braided hair and traveller locks, all of which are still markers of difference from mainstream culture.

Cutting hair is an equally problematic habit, and has varying social meanings beyond Olivelle's conclusions for Asia. In some cultures, cutting one's hair is seen as a sign of rebelliousness, whilst the lengthening of it has other connotations. In America, daughters within migrant Indian communities who cut their hair against the wishes of their father, cause considerable family disquiet. This is believed to be a rebellious activity and thus signals a loss of power to the head of the family (B. D. Miller 1998: 285). Olivelle regards shaved heads to mean anything from disempowerment to mourning, shame, sequestration, renunciation, and punishment (Olivelle 1998: 17–20). As examples are restricted to Asia, he does not discuss the fact that a close shaved head can also be practical, an aesthetic choice, a register of right wing political extremism or simply a gesture of personal non-conformity. Nor does he mention power and hair in relation to the military. In the US, for instance, new male military recruits have their hair cut short to signal co-option into another sphere of life, and submission to uniformity and authority.

The particular focus of this section is hairstyling associated with African American communities, a shifting cultural practice that has moved ground from a powerfully politicised practice – what Ryle calls 'trichological politics'

– that is an affirmation of black culture, to something more likely to be a personal statement (Ryle 2000: 18). In the 1960s, some blacks in America began to reject styles of beautification imposed on them by whites. Instead of 'relaxed' or process-straightened hair, they wore the unstraightened 'Afro', or what was called hair 'au naturel'. This came to be a sign of black power and identified with the militant black protest movement (Kelley 1997: 344). The political symbolism of hairstyling was encouraged by media exposure of a number of high profile 'Afro' wearers, including Jesse Jackson and even the young Michael Jackson. In fact there is a longstanding narrative of the 'Afro' hairstyle, which is not strictly African, that links it to masculine iconography and the potent symbolism of black power. Ironically, in the early years it was mostly women who wore natural hair, although Craig argues it was easier for men to do this, for women had to contend with more entrenched cultural views about beauty (Craig 1997: 411).

In the early 1970s, the 'Afro' began to lose its specific ideological meanings connected to urban rebellion. African Americans, including the post-black power generation of feminists, began to explore other decorative forms of hairstyle, plaits, waxes, beads, weaves and so on (Ryle 2000: 18). They built on past practices but changed their hair dressing from the long 'Afro' to the close-cut 'fro', introducing beads and plaited braids as fashion accessories (Kelley 1997: 349). Even so this was still a 'politicised' challenge to white gendered conventions about femininity, beautification and long hair, and continued to be regarded as an inappropriate form of ethnic pride by employers at the time. Even in 2001 Franklin, an African American woman, working in the UK, argues that 'Afros' and other forms of braids and locks were still a risky choice for a black woman (Franklin 2001: 146).

But by the late 1970s hair was increasingly being treated more as a style commodity, being plaited in corn-rows and fades, a flock wall paper effect that was worn as much in America and Britain, as in West Africa (Ryle 2000: 18). At the same time interesting issues of hybridity began to manifest themselves, both in relation to terminology, and in terms of style. Thus extensions of straight hair, added onto African American curly hair, can almost be regarded as a metaphor of cross-cultural assimilation. According to Ryle, Harlem hairdressers began to advertise braiding with African names like Casamance and Senegalese, while in Ghana hairdressers were labelling styles with US names such as Grace Jones, Cincinatti Boy and Boeing 707. Interestingly, from the 1990s young people in African cities started to appropriate Afro-American styles to dress their own hair. Ignoring meanings about resistance, they deliberately reconstituted these styles in their own ways as stylish, local African adornment (Biaya 1998: 91–2) (Figure 20). In another example, African American beaded or braided hair, worn by tennis aces Venus and Serena Williams, has taken the ethnic meanings of black hairdressing to a new register, one of worldwide celebrity significance.

Black hairstyling has a wide lexicon of terms and remains significant as a generalised sign of ethnic origins, but has become as much fashion as ideology. A substantial number of names and descriptions are associated with 'black' hair. Apart from better known terms such as 'dreds', braiding and cornrows, terms include bantu knots, bal'heads, afro puffs, tramlines, curly-perm, African plaits and so on, demonstrating its diversity as a social practice. In May 2001, the Victoria and Albert Museum in London organised 'A Day of Record'. On this day they invited men, women and children in the metropolitan area, blacks as well as non-blacks, associated by extension with the African Diaspora, and with black inspired hairstyles and nail art, to help document black British culture.[3] The event is an acknowledgement of the intense bearing this aspect of identity has on the dressed body. A

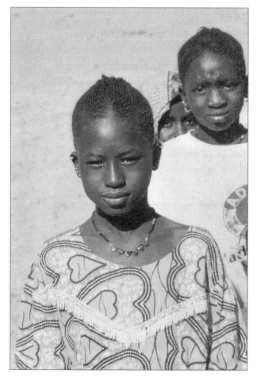 

20 Two young Foulani girls at Mopti, Mali 2003. Their hair is intricately braided, and one of them wears a loose fitting, brightly coloured local print outfit (in some places referred to as a *chitenge* outfit), of a type common to the regions of West Africa

21 Midge Purcell, her hair twisted with foils, participant at the Victoria and Albert Museum Day of Record, 2001

large number of people agreed to be photographed for the archive, now located in the Museum. Some of these subjects recorded interesting comments about what their own specific style of hairdressing meant for them. Many women felt braided and twisted hair was easy to manage, suited their daily activities, was slightly creative or 'different'. Of only a few who mentioned links to African heritage was a young woman called Midge Purcell, with twisted hair and foil decoration (Figure 21). She is recorded as saying, 'I chose this style as an expression of my African heritage, also, after years of using chemicals to straighten, curl or relax my hair, with unsatisfactory results, not to mention the constant expense, I finally decided to go "natural". I've never looked back'. So the 'Afro' is now a global style, one of many forms of commodified hairdressing, whose links to any original meanings are extremely tenuous.

A very noticeable subgroup of African American inspired hairstyles are 'dreadlocks', a style made popular by the reggae singer Bob Marley and popularised by his 1975 song 'Natty (knotty) Dread'. The origin of the style is not entirely clear. Some claim it lies in the 1930s and the founding of the Afro-Caribbean religion Rastafarianism that seeks a spiritual return to its African roots (Cox 1999: 224). Others say it comes from the rope-like hair of the Baye Fall sect in Senegal or the Asante priests in Ghana (Ryle 2000: 18). *Sadhu* in India also have similar locks, which are grown to great lengths. The term 'dreadlocks' may have been adopted to offend non-believers with an aversion to the look. Rastas outlaw the combing or cutting of the hair, and wear long twisted dreadlocks underneath knitted caps of red, gold and green as a sign of their affiliation (Wilson 1985: 199). Importantly, by the 1980s many non-Rastafarian blacks had begun to wear 'dreds' and knitted 'tams' as fashionable wear, and the style was also incorporated into white culture in the same decade (Cox 1999: 226). From the early 1990s 'Dreds', as a self-conscious style that promoted an unkempt, supposedly natural image, became a signature style for 'alternative' lifestyle practitioners, 'New Age' travellers and festival goers (see Figure 23, chapter 7).

Since then, 'dreds' have become transformed into a highly commodified style, worn by young people across all races as a mild form of 'alternative' to mainstream fashion. The 'look' has its own products, shampoos, beeswax, dreading combs and beads and hemp oil. There are even dreadlock websites offering advice on how to dress the hair.[4] If the right kind of hair cannot be grown, synthetic 'pseudo-dreds' can be grafted onto heads and called 'African' or 'Nubian' locks, entirely reconceptualising the original meanings of the style. Snowboarders, musicians, students and others now commonly wear them to create a 'look' without the pain of other kinds of alternative attire such as body piercing.

Importantly the 'Afro', and black style generally, has been about self-assertion and group identity. O'Neal argues that among African Americans, style as aesthetic expression has had the power to express cultural community as well as make bold statements about individuality. Appearance functions as a resistance to the mainstream and thus as a transforming element that shapes African Americans into a common culture. 'Style, then becomes a way of rejecting dominating myths, controlling the expressive shaping of one's immediate and everyday life, as well as holding on to one's past history' (O'Neal 1999: 132). In a survey of a broad spectrum of the community both educated and uneducated, she quotes one young woman saying that 'African Americans want this flashy look ... even with hairstyles; it matches the clothes ... The clothing is usually ... something that no one else has or if they have it, they'll change it up ... we'll always pick something that's really going to make us stand out and be noticed' (O'Neal 1999: 133). Where a black woman might feel reluctant to demonstrate signs of ethnicity in her work day clothing and hairstyling (Cox 1999: 144), the Afro and dreadlock hair style is now used by countless groups of people with little if any specific connection to black culture. This form of dress has acquired a more diffused set of meanings that speak quite eloquently to a global audience about individuality and a soft resistance to mainstream dressing.

Headscarves

Headscarves have been used, in different ways, to wrap the heads of women and men across traditional regional and modern cultures, all over Europe and throughout the Middle East. Its meanings are multifarious. In the developed world women who have lost their hair after chemotherapy wear scarves, men and women workers wear them for practical reasons, and they are a signature of 'Sloane Ranger' style. Even the bridal veil is a version of the headscarf. So veils can be as much a stylish accessory, as a traditional garment. Whilst they have many interpretations, the intention here is to focus in particular on questions of identity and the politics of the Muslim veil within a global perspective. The term headscarf or *hijab* will be used in preference to 'veil'. Recent scholarly writing on the subject of head coverings suggests that the term 'veil' is a controversial one, having no single Arab linguistic referent. It has many meanings and is one often adversely associated with western Orientalism (El Guindi 1999: xi and 6). El Guindi prefers to use the culturally specific term *hijab* to denote head coverings worn for reasons of modesty by Arab women.[5] Other authorities suggest that the term *hijab* describes a more self-consciously Islamic ident-ification, whilst headscarf is the term best suited to the loose *dupatta* head covering associated with South Asian forms of dress such as the *shalwar kameez* (Dwyer 1999: 22).

Although women are required to be modest in attire, the Quran does not proscribe in detail how women should dress, thus the precise appearance of Muslim headscarfs and amount of body covering varies according to culture and preference. Indeed the headscarf has many roles. Originally a traditional garment, the headscarf increasingly has modern application and also political ramifications. Paradoxically it can be a symbol of the progressively secular but also one of religious adherence. It can stand for tradition but equally be a sign of resistance (El Guindi 1999: 172). Some women feel it protects them from the gaze of men, and is thus liberating, offering them choice and even control over their lives. So whilst the *hijab* seems unquestionably to denote Islam, religious fundamentalism and repression for women, it can also be an expression of assertiveness, or an ideological commitment. If we take the modern Turkish Republic as an example, we find the headscarf (called a *türban* after the 1980s) is worn for a wide range of reasons linked to Muslim identity and politics, rural values, modesty, freedom of expression and religious idealism. It is variously a garment central to traditional rural life; marketed as a modest but decorative commodity for the Islamic urban middle class; worn by urban religious fundamentalists with the black, body enveloping *çarsaf*; and as a colourful scarf by secular modernists pro freedom of expression (Breu and Marchese 2000: 27–30). So it is used for a number of different reasons and can even be a fashionable item, for designer Islamic wear is one of the options for Muslim women.[6]

Hijab wearing is a global form of attire for Muslims but is also used by many western women living in Islamic countries who wear it out of cultural respect for Islam. It appears to visibly divide the world into those who use it and those who do not. Growing numbers of young Muslim women who live in the west choose it as a sign of modesty, pride in their faith and as a link to their cultural identity. But research indicates it has unstable and multifarious meanings. Dwyer shows that in a country like the UK, overdetermined dichotomies are set up between *hijab* wearers and those who do not, tending to polarise views about Muslim women, their class, gender and their conduct. This means women have to negotiate their personal position on Muslim dress, even challenge or rework its dominant understandings and meanings (Dwyer 1999: 6). Some young women interviewed by Dwyer, and who attended school, experimented with wearing headscarves on some days and not others. She interpreted this as 'strategic' wearing in order to negotiate public spaces (Dwyer 1999: 20–1). Others tried out different ways of tying them. Dwyer was struck by the confidence with which possible new British Muslim identities were being tried out in the various ways the headscarf was utilised.

Interestingly the veil has been introduced back into a number of Islamic countries having died out as a cultural habit. It was a second generation of women in Algeria after the war of independence who, in an effort to assert their Muslim identity, or who discovered Muslim values later in life, expressed this with the use of the foulard or scarf (MacMaster and Lewis 1998: 125). In the late 1570s the Islamic resistance movement in Palestine, Hamas, endeavoured to initiate *hijab* wearing especially amongst educated women in urban areas. The *hijab* had no precedent in Palestinian dress and was thus an introduced item of clothing, being an attempt to reinstate Islamic tradition and construct a particular and symbolic role for women (MacMaster and Lewis 1998: 173–4).

In the secular state of Turkey since the early 1980s, when regulations banned it from official government places such as universities, attempts to reintroduce the veil have been located at the centre of quite violent religious and social dissent (Breu and Marchese 2000: 25). Its popular use has proved highly contentious (Norton 1997: 169–70). For instance an interesting incident occurred in May 1999 when the newly elected Merve Kavakci, member of the Islamist Virtue Party, wore her headscarf at her parliamentary swearing in ceremony. The Chief Public Prosecutor had her evicted and applied to the Constitutional Court to have the Party disbanded. The event caused a political and public uproar, for the wearing of scarves was regarded as an assault on the secular state itself.[7] It has proved contentious in Egypt too, where those not using it have been harassed and accused of accepting of the seductive lure and sexual mores of American clothing (Zuhur 2001: 4). Yet the issue is complicated. In 1994, the Egyptian government tried to prevent *hijab* wearing in schools, unless with parental agreement, whilst the schools themselves encouraged it. A different situation has occurred in Singapore, where government schools have actually suspended girls wearing the traditional *tudung* scarf to school (Lyall 2002: 8).

Headscarves can be impediments to life in a predominantly western culture, especially evident since the 'War Against Terrorism'. They are provocative and attract particular condemnation and racial stereotyping. This makes it difficult for many Moslem women to participate fully in daily life, to gain employment or to play sport, and can cause problems for those trying to integrate.[8] In August 2000 a Danish retailer banned a young girl of Iraqi descent from wearing her headscarf whilst on work experience. The headscarf allegedly violated store dress codes, was thought to be unhygienic and offended customers. The girl took her case to the Danish High Court who found in her favour.[9] Employers have banned headscarves in other European countries, such as the Netherlands.

Within the global context, whether worn in a western or non-western culture the scarf brings difficulties with its wearing. It has become an emotive garment and increasingly politicised. Like hairdressing, the headscarf has a tendency to provoke reactive thinking and is part of the way differences between the Middle East and 'The West' are polarised (Lindisfarne-Tapper and Ingham 1997: 17). Cultural critics first noticed the media's particular hostility to it in press coverage of Saudi Arabia after the Gulf War and in Iran after the Iranian revolution of 1979 (El Guindi 1999: xi). With the Taliban administration of Afghanistan, this hostility was focused on their treatment of Afghan women. MacMaster and Lewis claim the media deliberately chooses to exaggerate images of heavy veiling in the reporting of religious fundamentalism, thereby constructing a view of the practice as excessive and barbaric (MacMaster and Lewis 1998: 129). van Dijk reports a similar situation in Indonesia with the *cadar*, or full face covering, where the degree of media emphasis seems out of sync with the limited numbers of women who wear it (van Dijk 1997: 75).

As a fuller understanding of Taliban practices emerge in the aftermath of the 'War Against Terrorism', 2001–2, these arguments may well be reinforced, or perhaps revised. Certainly the headscarf, and especially full body covering, or *burqua*, as worn by Taliban women took on a more sinister cast for the west after the terrorist attacks of September 11 2001. Some significant problems also arose for Muslim women who wore the *hijab* in non-Muslim countries. In an article on Muslim head scarves, the *Guardian* of 24 September quoted the words of Shagufta Yaqub, the 25-year-old editor of Q-News, Europe's biggest Muslim magazine. She said that many of her friends had been harassed or attacked while wearing the *hijab* and that this clothing, a sign of modesty, pride in religion and a signal of identity, made Muslim women extremely visible and thus vulnerable: 'We have considered, if this is a time of war, whether we should wear hats instead and play down our Islamic identity' (O'Sullivan 2001: 2). So the scarf, like many other forms of dress, is superficially a global style, yet at the same time it is a localised garment, which can sometimes be subject to individual choice and preference. In the precise manner of its wearing, in selection of colour and fabric, it is a form of dress that still allows many Muslim women a degree of opportunity to negotiate their particular place within a larger social framework, although it can also be a dangerous stereotype.

Hats

Although wearing hats has largely died out as an everyday convention for men and women in urban cultures all over the world, they continue to be used as practical or protective garments. Some forms of hat or cap can be regarded as almost universal, such as the hard hat, the towelling hat (Kangol) or the knitted 'beanie'. This is also the case with the popular baseball cap, which some might say personifies the 'American way of life', but is now worn in every part of the globe. Headwear also plays a significant official role as part of the uniform of law enforcement agents, the military and in group or team solidarity. So for a range of reasons hats are highly visible social indicators, more immediately noticeable perhaps than other forms of attire. Aside from formal headwear, fads and trends in hats are equally significant indicators, now with global rather than local application. One such case is the baseball cap popularly worn backwards. This is a style linked to homeboy and homegirl culture and a 'cheap and stylish source of fantasies of Americanicity' (Ross 1994: 288). Worn in reverse it is, Ross claims, no longer a catchy affectation, but part of the iconography of social crisis, perhaps the first truly global symbol of youth.[10] This may have been the case in the mid-1990s, but the style has been widely appropriated by other social levels. It is, for example, the signature style of tennis ace Lleyton Hewitt. As such it is beamed by the media to every part of the globe, thus cementing a new level of meaning for the garment.

But hats also operate on very local forms of register. They have particular meanings associated with social affiliations, regional folk cultures, gender, and ethnic groups and often accrue national symbolism. We associate the tall pointed hat with Wales, the *peci* with Indonesia and the beret with France. So the overarching nature of global everyday hat wearing can be challenged by diversionary tactics or subject to negotiated difference as well. For instance, baseball caps are not entirely generic, they can be customised with group or personal logos and motifs. So they are implicated in changes that take place between normative conventions or structures of a social system, and the subtle reorientations made by individuals when constituting new sets of social circumstances.

Styles of hat can migrate around the world, accruing meaning as they are taken up and assimilated by different cultures. The male bowler is an example of a British style taken over by South American women, in a curious appropriation of style but not meaning. The bowler is identifiable as the attire of London city 'gents' who work in banking, the civil service or the professions, or just those who wish others to think they are part of this world (Robinson 1993: 166). Whilst bowler hat wearing has declined substantially since the 1980s, its wearing was not confined to Britain. What is intriguing is that Andean *cholas*, native women from Ecuador to Chile, some of whom have moved to the towns, wear similar headgear and it is especially popular on the Bolivian altiplano, and among the Aymara and Quechua people. So why was the male bowler hat (sometimes it is a sort of derby or trilby) taken over by Andean women, and men too? How did this form of headwear come to have other meanings in respect of class and nationality? According to Robinson, when British workers, of

22 Two elderly men, sitting in the Plaza de Armas, Cuzco, wearing predominantly western style clothing and footwear but with local hats, the latter derivative of the European trilby

urban origin, arrived in Bolivia in the 1920s to build the railroads they brought these hats with them. Native Andean women, as well as men, took to wearing them and they are now locally made in a variety of colours (Figure 22). An account by a western visitor to the region in 1990 suggests the wearing of the hats by *chola* women is a calculated statement. They are neither practical, nor warm and often several sizes too small. Thus: 'They seem like a deliberate effort to dress up, to assert a cultural identity; even to mock the foreigners who introduced the hats in the first place' (Robinson 1993: 170). Perhaps this is an imagined intention, but these garments do show that style evolves and can be migratory. Hats can be produced and can function in different parts of the world at much the same time and signify entirely different things.

The complex meanings attached to hats are illustrated by the Australian Akubra, or so called 'Aussie' bush hat. This was originally worn chiefly by working men in the country, but later taken up by women and urban dwellers. Whilst the Akubra has fascinating similarities to American Western cowboy gear, discussed below, the hat nevertheless embodies a series of nostalgic and mythic qualities associated with Australianness, masculinity, legendary stockmen and rural life.[11] What more stunning example could one find of this mythology than the energetic phalanx of Akubra-wearing rough riders who burst into Sydney's Stadium Australia, signalling the commencement of the Opening Ceremony of the 2000 Olympic Games. A complicating factor is that indigenous people have adopted the Akubra as a symbol of indigenous solidarity. Men and women activists for the indigenous cause wear a black Akubra with a hatband in the black, red and gold colours of the indigenous flag, taking inspiration from the dress of indigenous stockmen of the past. It is difficult to describe this headwear as a national costume, but like the poni, the Akubra hat has connotations that link it to clothing of the 'common man', whether Aussie bushman or indigenous activist.

But as a sign of globalisation, Akubra hats are not simply sold by Australians to Australians, they are marketed and popular worldwide. Akubra is a brand with agents all over USA, Canada, New Zealand, Africa and the Middle East; Stetson have also made Akubra under licence, showing solid evidence of the hybrid nature of manufacturing. So the Akubra is a fine example of global branding, but capitalises on the importance of connections to local Australian identity, 'genuineness' and a simple but hard rural life.[12] The product demonstrates Appadurai's conceptualisation of the way in which 'the local', can become a kind of fetish that obscures the real nature of global or transnational production methods, and thus of global consumption as well (Appadurai 1996: 42). One of the interesting points Appadurai makes in considering today's temporal rhythms of consumption, is that mass marketeers inculcate in consumers an ersatz nostalgia for the past or bygone lifestyles to fuel consumer desires (Appadurai 1996: 76). This applies to the Akubra as it does to the marketing of jeans. But, as he suggests, companies don't expect the consumer to provide the memory, rather they teach consumers to miss things they never had, via what he calls 'imagined nostalgia'.

The whole issue of meanings attached to the Akubra is complicated by the love/hate relationship Australia has with American popular culture, thus demonstrating how cultural symbols migrate across national borders. The hat's popularity can partly be attributed to a taste for rural sports, especially rodeos, and ways it is linked with the growing popularity of Country and Western music, According to Hoy the Australian stockman actually looks to the American cowboy for validation, despite the greater harshness of the Outback and the daring riding practices of bushmen. Hoy maintains the benchmark for Australian rodeos is defined by the American version. The reason he suggests is that America has more successfully romanticised and propagandised nostalgia for the rugged days of the wild west, in contrast to Australia, although life in the Outback is far more testing. The Australian stockman lives a life that the open-range cowboys used to live, a life that is only a nostalgic dream to American cowboys (Hoy 2000: 208–10). All these meanings feed back into consumption and marketing. Ironically it seems the popularity of the Akubra hat has been fuelled by dreams of an imagined rural past characteristic of another country. This has been fuelled by the Wild West movie industry, American style rodeos, as well as by Australian mythmaking and films with Australian content like Crocodile Dundee.

Hairstyles, hats and headwear are items of dress and body adornment with particularly potent, complex and often localised meanings. But whereas in the past their meanings were linked quite specifically to nation, class and status, in the global world these signs are likely to be more diffuse and migratory. Investments of meanings may shift dialectically from the specificity of regionalism to a worldwide generality, as power, status and ethnic affiliations themselves change, or are subject to international modernisation or diasporic shifts. As with 'Afro' hairstyles, they can convey multiple or hybrid messages, be subject to change and negotiation as cultures shift, assimilate and then reform again. A hat can be made in one part of the world and have fairly local meanings, but carry entirely different social messages dependent on who wears it and the new circumstances in which it is worn. An item of headwear such as the *hijab* in one context can be a radical gesture, in another a practical garment for protection and in another environment can be a sign of orthodoxy. In addition to this, many items of headwear have been co-opted by fashion and their original meanings blurred, altered or even lost entirely. So understanding dress for the head in a global environment requires us to be alert to new readings. We may need to reconsider entirely its original function, its significance, its rationale, as well as past models of comprehension.

Notes

1 Fieldwork among the Tuareg was undertaken by Rasmussen in 1983.

2 The red headband has historical links to the *bonnet rouge* worn by militants during the French Revolution.

3 Information comes from the Press Release for 'A day of record. Nails, weaves and naturals: black British hairstyles and nail art', 7 May 2001, and associated on-line archival material in the Victoria and Albert Museum.

4 See www.dreadlocks.com, accessed February 2002.

5 Other writers use the word foulard, or kerchief, and the term *jilbab* is used by writers on Indonesian clothing to describe a Muslim woman's long costume plus her head covering (van Dijk 1997: 75).

6 See The Complete Hijab website for designer wear, (http://members.aol.com/ RvrGdnArts/hijab-a.htm, accessed October 2001).

7 BBC News, 7 May 1999. http://news.bbc.co.uk/hi/english/world/europe/newsid _337000/337361.htm, accessed October 2001.

8 To assist Muslim women in Holland and elsewhere with the practical problems of veil wearing, Cindy van den Bremen, from Eindhoven in the Netherlands, designed a series of modern styles of head covering, suitable for activities like tennis, gym

and skateboarding. These were produced after consultation with Muslim women and an Imam. http://www.isim.nl/newsletter/4/general/3.html, 10 January 2000, accessed April 2001. The design suitable for tennis is a garment that looks like the wimple of a nun, covers the head tightly and extends over the shoulders but leaves the face free.

9 10 European Industrial Relations On-line (eiro), 28 August 2000. http://217.141.24.196/2000/08/Feature/DK0008192F.html, accessed July 2001.

10 It has been alleged that outfielder Ken Griffey Jr of the Seattle Mariners was the first to encourage young baseball players to turn their hats around.

11 The different types of hat are closely matched with rural terminology, like Cattleman, Snowy River, Stockman, Bronco, Pastoralist, and Territory.

12 Akubra was named as an Australian brand of the year in 1996, and in 1998 was one of twenty so-called Icon products, including Dryza-Bone, Speedo and R. M. Williams.

7 ✧ What's the alternative?

The girl's name is Jude. I had the Thunderbolt in sub-light warp-drive when I saw her, but I would have stopped for her any day! She was lovely, though I suppose I shouldn't be expressing these heretical sentiments: after all, we are all asexual these days. (Description of a Kuranda 'hippie' near Nimbin, New South Wales, in 1973, Jiggens 1983)

How are people experiencing the nature of this new reality – the rising of the depth currents of all times, all cultures, and all experiences? Its effects are felt in the fascination with myth, the seeking of spiritual experience ... styles of clothing that mix and match continents on a single body ... Today, and for all of us, all parts of the planet are catching all parts of the planet. (Houston 1996)

ALTHOUGH dress in the developed world exists in proximity to, and sometimes in antagonism to, varied interactions and discourses of 'difference', namely regional, subcultural, national, religious and ethnic, there is in global dressing, as we have seen, a strong element of generic sameness. There is also a clearly defined counter discourse to this, even though its characteristics have moved closer to mainstream clothing since the early 1990s. It is sometimes labelled 'alternative' dress, a term which also embraces body decoration such as piercing and tattoos. This clothing is central to the formation of identity amongst so called 'New Age' social groupings in the US, the UK, Europe, Asia and Australia, and increasingly worn by backpackers and a slightly radical subset of mainstream dressers. So it is constituted by the dress of the more philosophically committed plus a milder form which, for the present purposes, is termed 'alternative' dress, although the terms can be used interchangeably. Whilst still subject to a degree of personal choice, both forms are composed of fairly predictable and generally agreed sets of components, manifestly different from generic everyday dress. With some minor exceptions, clothing of this kind can be said to show a conformity of non-conformity.

The purpose of this chapter is to consider 'New Age' and 'alternative' dressing, and to question their place in a globalised but fragmented world. One could argue that mainstream clothing is itself one of the factors responsible for creating the need for an alternative, a perceived certainty of identity. Importantly both ways of dressing function in relationship to the global. The perspective brought to this chapter is that despite the conformity, some subtle changes are shown over time, and certain aspects of these practices vary slightly in different parts of the world. In Australia, for example, there are ways in which the construct of 'Aboriginality' informs a range of local 'New Age' rhetorics, appropriations and beliefs about the land. Even so the variations are less evident in precise articles of dress, than in the false idealisation of, and reaching out to, indigenous culture by 'New Age' people (Newton 1988: 67). The question is, does 'alternative' dress continue to symbolise resistance, as it did in the 1970s, has it been co-opted into the mainstream or does it lie somewhere in between?

There has been much debate, among theorists within cultural studies, art history and anthropology, about the construct of the 'primitive', said to be both a distortion of, and a form of insulation from, the realities of cultural differences (Clifford 1992; Klesse 2000; Rosenblatt 1997; Torgovnick 1990). As part of this concept, lies the dressing of those who are sometimes called 'Modern Primitives'. These non-mainstream consumers demonstrate in various ways a distinction between their own believed 'authentic' desires, including attire, and those supposedly inauthentic ones considered to be endemic to western capitalism. What they do is to enact their beliefs ritually by invoking the idea of the primitive in terms of dress, tattoos and so on (Rosenblatt 1997: 324–5). Klesse argues that this romantically idealises 'primitivism', thereby simply reinforcing the stereotypical dichotomy between western culture and the 'other', and does little to upset the practices and discourses of the status quo (Klesse 2000: 34–5). This dress which consciously offers itself as a conceptual and material alternative to mainstream attire, but at the same time appropriates and consumes indigenous motifs and 'tribal' styles, offers a particularly complex relationship to the 'primitive other', although it is increasingly indicative of style over substance. For instance 'alternative' consumers have a fascination with 'authentic' or hand made commodities, and a deep-seated attraction to the 'ethnic' products of first nation peoples. These include those of North America, South America, subcontinental Indians, Indonesians and Australian Aborigines. But this kind of dress cannot be entirely separated out from everyday global consumption, so the complicated nature of 'alternative' shopping and its points of association with 'ethnic chic' (see chapter 5) are considered.

New tribes?

In 1994–95 Matthew Sleeth took a series of photographs entitled 'The New Tribes', showing groups of men, women and children occupying the beautiful, fertile areas of Nimbin and Mullumbimby, near to World Heritage listed Nightcap Mountain National Park, (Northern New South Wales, Australia).[1] His image of 'Alan, Meri and three children' (Figure 23) forms part of this series. Both these adults are characteristically dressed, with tangled hair, and Meri wears a loose slip with an 'ethnic' style print shawl over her shoulder. As such they are representative of many people who have settled on the immediate rural edges of large metropolitan centres, in areas carefully chosen for their aesthetic, supposedly spiritual qualities. Although there are part-time urban counterparts, 'New Age' people have traditionally had a preference for sequestering themselves away from city life, escaping to some form of allegedly benign pre-modern existence, demonstrating yearning for an 'authenticity' they believe adheres to designated rural sites. 'New Age' people are not necessarily agrarian, although numerous groups and communities do work the land. Many were, and indeed still are nomads, living permanently on the road. Alternatively they travel far from their places of origin to remote, supposedly untouched countries like Nepal and Tibet. Many, like 'Alan and Meri', are associated with bands, in this case the Earth Reggae Group. Such people are repeatedly drawn to rock and other music festivals; the commercial Glastonbury

23 Alan, Meri and three children practising the 'alternative' way of life, 1994–95

Festival (first held in 1970), the free Stonehenge festival of the midsummer solstice (1974–85), festival/raves such as at Castlemorton, Gloucestershire (1992), the Queensland Maleny Folk Festival (from 1985 – resited and renamed the Woodford Folk Festival in 1994), its associated Murri Festival, the annual Nimbin Mardi Grass hemp festival, the Rainbow Tribe gatherings all over the US and Europe, as well as numerous country markets around the world.

Groups of people such as these live in buses, caravans or teepees, hair in dreadlocks or with shaved heads, men bearded, in loin cloths, women in tie dye clothes, loose dresses, some bare breasted, others with peasant-like headscarves and hand blocked shawls. Some have face markings and mohican hair. Sometimes called 'New Age' travellers, 'Neo-Pagans' or 'Drop Outs', they are gypsy wanderers originating mainly from cultures in the developed world. Their easily identifiable clothing often shows a disregard for orthodoxy and notions of neatness, with an obsession for 'first nation' cultural products. These ingredients are collaged together to create a recognisable identity for the wearers, a form of transnational identity, but one representing a very distinct difference from the mainstream. Their clothing and associated body marking generally have an unspecific 'ethnic' flavour, a curious mixture of concern with personal identity but primarily as it relates to their 'tribe' or group.

Terminology

The terms 'alternative', 'New Age' and counter-culture need some analysis, for their meanings have been widely debated.[2] One should not assume that 'alternative' or counter-cultural necessarily means youthful. In fact Janice Newton quotes data from the Melbourne *Age* newspaper that suggests in 1987 one fifth of estimated 'alternative stylers' were over fifty (Newton 1988: 55). The use of the word 'alternative' in relation to clothing is also less than straightforward. A search of the internet reveals so called 'alternative clothing' can comprise anything from Gothic subcultural dress to rubber, lace and PVC clothing, or gear for cross dressers. On the other hand it can simply mean clothing sold on line rather than department store clothing, with 'alternative' referring to the method, or point of sale, not the clothing itself.

The counter-culture of the 1960s, including the 'hippie' subculture, is the origin of the later 'alternative lifestyler'. The term is sometimes used interchangeably with 'New Age', the latter a vague one with origins in Britain in the 1880s and associated early on with Dayspring Theosophy (Roe 1997–8: 172). In the 1960s, being part of the counter-culture was to deliberately separate from the parent culture, drawing on Eastern mysticism, Green politics, political Leftism and communality, to shape concepts of dress, music and attitudes of behaviour. The distinctiveness of hippie culture subsequently fragmented in several directions, one of the most obvious being the 'Utopian alternative culture' (Clarke *et al.* 1981: 73). The term 'counter-cultural' thus implies an ideology of disaffection, albeit not explicitly political, and a body of ideas to which youth committed in order to signal a precise break from middle-class life. It is worth noting that in 1981 Clarke *et al.* could still argue that this disaffection was strategically placed within the dominant class, thus enabling the critique to be launched from within a privileged class position (Clarke *et al.* 1981: 76).

The issue of the 'alternative' life, and its relation to class, is significant. The original notion of dissatisfaction with middle-class life has subsequently been reshaped. This has occurred through a series of different historical waves of lifestyle activity. Radical aspects of 'hippie' lifestyle were softened in the 1980s. The notion that being a successful consumer was to be essentially individualistic, helped to allow 'alternative style' to become something more generally accepted, and less of a class based form of 'dropping out'. In 1976 it was estimated 95 per cent of Australia's 'drop outs' were in fact middle-class, urban dwellers (Lindblad 1976a: 32). They could be students, drifters or tired, former advertising executives, looking to share the symbols and activities implied by the term. In the UK they have come as much from a working-class as a middle-class background. But, according to Hetherington, by identifying with a series of different ethnicities which they regard as classless, they leave behind both their settled lives and whatever links they had to class (Hetherington 2000: 105). More recently, the increasingly disordered nature and less rigid attitudes of mainstream society, and the triumph of capitalism over welfare politics has altered the dogmatically antithetical, anti-consumptionist and fully ideological aspect of earlier counter-cultural ideas, with their strong resistance to middle-class mores. These have evolved into more subjective core values, such as individual freedom and self-identity, especially those of spirituality and personal growth. Certain vague beliefs about environ-mental ethics, and the hand made have come to colour 'New Age' philosophies, and labels such as 'hippie' have become derogatory. Softer terms such as 'alternative lifestylers', 'New Age travellers', 'Neo-Pagans' and even 'ferals' are commonly in use.

Maffesoli, in his book *The Time of the Tribes* (1996), argues that in the late twentieth century, mass culture had fragmented and disintegrated, with the resulting dispersion of overall social cohesion. He argued that consumer culture had become a series of different tribes. These communities could be characterised by fluidity, role-playing and theatricality, more focused on spectacle than other affiliations (Maffesoli 1996: 77). The classical stability of customary tribalism had been reconfigured in this *theatrum mundi* by the playing of games centred on appearance and the body, where everyone was both actor and spectator. Caroline Evans has questioned whether the term 'urban tribes' is appropriate to describe these cultural practices in postindustrial societies (Evans 1997: 172). But the notion of 'style tribes' has gained popular currency with publications like *Streetstyle* (1994) by Ted Polhemus. He loosely and unproblematically conflates the style of urban street dwellers, like punks, with indigenous and ethnic groups, gathering them all together in what he terms the 'Supermarket of Style' (Polhemus 1994: 130). A further point is that 'style tribalism', if it can indeed be so termed, manifests itself quite differently in cities from the rural based groups of the 'New Age'. Whilst we may query the terminology of 'tribe', Maffesoli's view that the performance of style is a crucial aspect of post industrial urban dress, is one that clearly explains current 'New Age' dress, where the spectacle of appearance increasingly encroaches on the philosophies that originally underpinned it. Young professionals, IT specialists and academics happily attend festivals wearing 'New Age' gear, and then return home to more mundane lives, and the often homogenised dress of the global environment.

Spatiality and time

'New Age' attire is not unchanging, and since the 1970s its alternations have mirrored those of other global consumption patterns. The variable nature of 'New Age' clothing supports Caroline Evans' model of subcultural identities and their style post 1970. She suggests we regard the earlier class based models of resistance by authors like Hebdige as intrinsically problematic. She favours a view of subcultures as fluid and 'unfixed', in a persistent state of 'becoming', seeing them as constantly mobile, engaging in a trafficking of style, and so travelling through various identifications. She concludes her essay by arguing that subcultures have become diasporic in their flight from fixity (Evans 1997: 185). Yet paradoxically, despite their state of perpetual change, the urban groups she studied remained largely static in relation to location. For various reasons, the issue of the dress of subcultures who are nomadic has escaped study. In part this present account seeks to redress this omission. 'New Age' patterns of wearing and associated behaviour are indeed transnational. For this reason they confound any model of subcultures as localised. They exhibit a form of attire that is parallel to global dress but a counterpoint to it, thus operating on a different register from the existing spatiality of global consumption.

Within the global arena, people and cultural objects with which they are related, are increasingly detached from specific localities. Migration, diasporic population movements and even tourism itself have contributed to the ways in which cultures are now increasingly seen to be 'impure' and disjointed. From this point of view, cultural diffusion and the hybridity of global population flows are challenging former localised forms of culture and straightforward dichotomous notions of 'home' and 'away', 'authentic' and 'contrived' (Rojek and Urry 1997: 4). Cultural theorists of time and space, such as Clifford and Lury, concerned with both the actual and metaphorical aspects of mobility, have extended thinking in this respect. Rejecting any notion of identity as fixed, and culture as 'uncontaminated' or sealed, they proffer dynamic comparative analyses of everyday cultures as sites of both dwelling and travel (Clifford 1992: 105 and Lury 1999: 76). Their theories, although differing in application, allow us to rethink the essential nature of culture in fluid ways, in what Clifford terms 'travelling-in-dwelling' and 'dwelling-in-travelling', 'passing-throughness', 'border crossings' and 'criss crossings'. All of this raises the question where do 'New Age' cultural wanderers, their appearances and bodily dispositions or habituses, even ethnicities, fit within our increasingly hybridised global environment? Do they remain fundamentally resistant in style and thus fully 'alternative'? In other words, do they entirely stand aside from normative consumption or is it merely consumption on a different register?

'New Age' groups and 'alternative' lifestyle adherents, dismiss current fashion by compiling dress and mannerisms culled from secondhand clothing and a range of cultures beyond their own (especially those of marginalised status or geographically distant, often indigenous cultures). Even those who occasionally wear 'alternative dress', but are not fully committed to it, stand against fashion's devotion to novelty, which they see as intrinsic to competitive materialism. They demonstrate a slowing down of consumption in the western sense, rejecting instantaneous, fast-paced metropolitan time, by occupying another slower, more muted time differential. They give evidence of a desire to get away (without always going away), or in some cases travel to places quite remote from urban centres. As Hetherington claims, the cultural politics of the 'New Age traveller way of living', is a politics of identity but also a spatial politics of freedom and authenticity (Hetherington 2000: 26). Whilst purporting to be classless (certainly coming from various classes) their sense of identity is one collaged together primarily from disparate ethnicities and marginalised first nation peoples. Indeed, says Hetherington, the margin is the basis of the traveller's sense of identity (Hetherington 2000: 94). I would differ somewhat from this view, suggesting that theirs is not so much a marginal identity, but rather a sense of communal difference, operating both from within, as well as from without, the mainstream.

Generally speaking counterculture and 'alternative style' is a distinctive and material manifestation of a collective style, or set of choices, made to signal the desire for difference, while simultaneously demonstrating a desire to retain a sense of personal identity and self-hood (Hetherington 2000: 93). Yet 'alternative' dressing is not random. It is dress and behaviour semiotically selected from a repertoire of items, and is subject to certain chosen dispositions. Although existing within distinct schemas and following certain prescribed parameters this 'look', in its insistence on almost reactionary modalities like long beards, loose hair and peasant headscarves, is deliberately challenging the mainstream (Figure 24). In other words this form of dress, sometimes labelled 'hippie' or 'feral', is a style of 'difference', yet it is also a style found worldwide and thus in certain ways quite uniform. Participants at a Stonehenge festival, for instance, are likely to be little different in their dress from those attending the Woodford Folk Festival in Australia. So it is possible to speak of 'New Age' dressing as a global style. As well, it clearly has points of reference to Retro fashion that nostalgically embraces the old, the forsaken, the supposedly individualistic, the hand made and the imperfect. The put together appearances of 'New Age' practitioners are thus made up of carefully chosen, hand picked secondhand clothes, hand downs, sometimes exchanged rather than purchased, 'seconds' or throw outs, and certain kinds of cheap, imported ethnic textiles and beads found widely at street markets. It is a trading cycle that is little studied.

24 A man with unusually long beard and hair, his black sweater inscribed 'calling all tribes'. His companion wears an 'alternative' style garment, decorated with a mandala symbol, Mullumbimby markets, New South Wales 2002

First wave

Demonstrating a complicated mix between conformity and change, 'New Age' dress has undergone certain changes since the 1970s. The first wave of anti-mainstream 'New Age' clothing emerged in Europe, America and Australia in the late 1960s with the dress of the 'hippie' subculture and continued to be worn throughout the 1970s. The terms first and second wave are used here fairly loosely. The intention is to suggest that certain shifts have occurred in attitudes and behaviours within alternative culture, despite many practices that have now become almost ritualised and which ignore social changes over time. Counter-cultural and 'alternative lifestyle' practitioners, the so called 'drop-outs' of the 1960s and early 1970s were at this period young, idealistic and environmentally conscious. Some students alarmed by the inhumanities of the Vietnam war and feeling unable to change mainstream society via the protest movement, felt that by living an alternative life, at least they could change themselves (Cock 1979: 215). They wanted to get away from the conformities of mainstream existence in order to cleanse their inner lives, express their feelings and reduce consumption.

The discussion that follows centres mainly on Australia, yet the attitudes and dress of alternative communities is remarkably similar wherever it occurs. So the Australian examples are taken to be broadly representative of similar patterns in other places. Starting with urban communes in Melbourne, groups soon began to venture further afield, moving north, and gradually settling around the Rainbow region of North Eastern New South Wales. Similar groups were forming in California. Others took to the hippie trail that went from southern parts of Australia to New South Wales and then to Cairns and Darwin. Others went further, budget trekking to Malaysia, Cambodia, Nepal and India, where they joined like minded young back-packers from the US, Canada, New Zealand and Europe. Although this essentially anti-mainstream attitude was a widespread phenomenon of mid century capitalist societies, there were, in places like Australia, local reson-ances (Newton 1988: 55). Newton claims that the counter-culture in Australia was largely derivative of America, although she feels the Australian version may have been quieter and less extreme (Newton 1988: 56). According to Jill Roe, Australasia is likely over time to have been more responsive to 'New Age' thinking than America (Roe 1997–8: 172). But the express degree to which Australia's 'New Age' movement was a replica of America still requires research (Roe 1997–8: 184).

Those who went to live in rural environments tried to be self sufficient, and live a non-competitive subsistence life in small communities resembling tribes, often ten to twelve people. They spearfished, did hand craft work, worked part-time, even made their own clothes (Cock 1979: 27). At a time of growing nationalist sentiment, John Lindblad put this down to a new spirit of appreciation for the countryside and as a way of hiding from 'the advancing and imposing pollution of an imported Anglo-American culture' (Lindblad 1976b: 77). In other countries it was more likely a general dislike of middle-class values and politics. Communities had strong philosophical beliefs favouring asexuality, and nudity was commonly practised. In a piece of investigative journalism for the *Bulletin* about 'Drop Outs' in Australia, written in 1976 and published in two parts, Lindblad included a number of illustrations of nudity being practised in communities and co-operatives all over Australia. The alternative media of small magazines, *Grass Roots* magazine, *Nimbin News* and others, strengthened this sense of community which included common forms of clothing, language and values (Cock 1979: 46–7). This sharing of resources and bartering was something mainstream society would scarcely contemplate. But people were not egalitarian. Although always subject to certain schemas of appearance and types of apparel, they aimed in many cases to dress in individualistic ways.

The energy in the early years was palpable. Inspired by rock music festivals and alternative theatre, ideas were garnered from African and Asian village life, from indigenous cultures generally, and from Eastern mysticism. An article by one lifestyler published in the modest, alternative broad sheet *Nimbin News*, aptly conveyed the mood of the period. This is something that could equally represent California and even parts of the UK at the time – 'We were a ragtag collection of gypsies – many free to be there because there was nothing else happening and pleasure was the promise, and that's where the flow was. Flowing and avoiding hassles' (Dunstan 1978: 10).

The Aquarius Festival at Nimbin, New South Wales, Australia's first alternative festival, was sponsored by the Australian Union of Students and the government Community Arts program in 1973, and was a version of the 1969 Woodstock Festival. It is a good example of the unstructured enthusiasm with which the notion of a 'different' way was espoused and celebrated. The vibrancy of ideas generated by the first Festival lasted a generation. Nimbin, a down-at-heel dairying area, was chosen as the site because it was an isolated rural area and lay in the shadow of Nimbin Rocks, a place of cultural significance for the Bundjalung Aboriginal people. Estimates of numbers attending vary from 5000 – 10,000. They came to join in the magic circles, the healing events, the street theatre, to listen to music and chanting and to consume vegetarian food. New spiritualised rituals were designed to replace old European ones that had grown stale, the deliberate recreation of 'tribal' structures, celebration of oneness with the earth and associated behaviours were a key element (Newton 1988: 59).

Clothing was not an important aspect of the ideology of the time and some practised a form of disinterest. Many groups professed to abhor material wealth, and demonstrated this by wearing jumble sale clothes, old and secondhand furs and army great coats, some of which continues to be a key part of Retro style thirty and more years later. Jeans were commonly worn, as were gum boots, colourful hand made shawls, tie dye T-shirts, hand knits, patchwork trousers, waistcoats, peasant blouses and sometimes checked shirts. Others wore farmer's clothing (Cock 1979: 113). Hair for men and women was long and sometimes uncared for. The general appearance of participants was an amalgam of army disposal gear, corduroy pants, flowing batik dresses, 'hippie chicks in their lacy velvet St Vinnie specials; fine cool cats in flared bell bottom jeans and leather tasselled vests; silent swamis and yogis; Hare Krisnas in their saffron robes braying their devotions ... the whole panoply of counter cultural Australia strolling through town ... with one question burning in their hearts – *What's happening man?'* (Jiggens 1983: 11).

The second wave

Many who attended the Nimbin Aquarius Festival found it so inspirational that they could not leave, and some still live there, or in surrounding areas. Over the years a great many further celebrations and festivals followed, like the Alternative Lifestyle Festival in 1978. Some, like the Nimbin Lifestyle Celebration Festival of 1983, sought nostalgically to revive the spirit of the first. The reputation of Nimbin as a cultural centre, a place of alternative experimentation and as a colourful environment endures. It remains Australia's 'alternative' culture capital, alive with artists, musicians and holistic medicine practitioners, but has altered in many ways.[3] It has become a town with an up market atmosphere and a haven for business. Andrew Thurtell described Nimbin's almost schizophrenic character in 2000, observing that 'Internet providers, solicitors and pizza shops sit alongside those selling earth bricks, hand woven Guatemalan textiles and organic food. It's hard to tell the difference between the real estate agency and the famous "Rainbow Café"' (*Sunday Mail* 2000: 4 June). This is where, in 1973, people ate together in peace and held hands; they were not thinking about their latest investment portfolio.

If we look around the world to other examples beyond Australia, we find similar evidence of marked changes toward entertainment rather than commitment. Many annual festivals are no longer free entry and are restricted to those with available cash. Some have disappeared or have re-emerged in changed form. Stonehenge, a place of pilgrimage and community, was crucial for formulating the identity of 'New Age' travellers between 1975 and 1986. After this time problems with squatting and other legal infringements caused travellers to be exiled from the site, a ruling that was relaxed slightly in 1998 but still without free access (Hetherington 2000: 152–3). The UK Criminal Justice Act of 1994, with its new laws of trespass, meant that many travellers gave up living in Britain and moved to the continent. There are, in fact, numerous gatherings recorded as having taken place in the US and Europe. For instance 'Rainbow Tribe' or 'Family' gatherings have taken place in Romania, Hungary, Portugal, the Czech Republic and in the US at such places as Mitchell and in the Ochococ National Forest, Oregon in 1997.[4]

It is common in mainstream society to term second wave 'alternative' dressing 'feral' clothing. But dividing 'alternative' dress categorically and somewhat artificially into periods is misleading. Although there has been a strong shift toward greater commodification of this kind of dress, and a form of trendy aestheticisation has emerged since the 1980s, the dress of 'New Age' travellers has, at times, remained faithful to earlier concepts. De la Haye and Dingwell illustrate the unkempt 'Donga Tribe Traveller dress' 1986–94, in their book on subculture clothing in the UK, some of which was worn at the first Solstice Festival at Stonehenge. These clothes show a recognisable and often repeated combination of layering of thread-bare items, passed down clothing, ethnic items, army surplus, hand made and patchwork articles (de la Haye and Dingwell 1996).

Although building on the dress of the first wave, 'New Age' attire since the 1990s has lacked its commitment to other values, being more integrated into the marketing system of globalisation. This evolution had been partly engendered by media interest, reducing it to trendiness, and converting 'alternative' into a commodified, respectable, even weekend fashion. Richard Neville explains the new mood in his lively book *Hippie Hippie Shake* (1996), arguing that the forest defender of the future is quite different from the past. He creates the vivid image; 'a feral at a lap top, I imagine, is surfing the net, organising a portside blockade of a shipment of wood chips'. In 1995, participating in the Byron Bay Festival, a small town not far from Nimbin, Neville felt a very strange sense of *deja vu*, as if experiencing an acid flashback or flash forward. He described the crowds as 'a nineties knees up for eco-dreamers … the costumes of a hundred cultures from punk to Pakistan, from an Edwardian circus to The Arabian Nights, are combined with stylish wit. Strangers smile, friends hug. This is a happy tribe I realise (Neville 1996: 359–60). He might also have said that this was a happy and performing tribe, a tribe at leisure, a tribe on a brief holiday from mundane city life. After the celebration had ended, most had to get back to everyday life and jobs in the city.

Certain kinds of 'ethnic' clothes and trinkets are manufactured on a mass scale to cater to the 'alternative' taste. In the 1970s there was less cynical sense that such attire was performative. This is not to say that counter-cultural dress was staid. But dress was worn with a degree of idealism, as a genuine expression of a particular philosophy. This has changed. Young people, and those not so young, consume 'alternative' attire as clothing in which they may have only minor personal or philosophical investment. It is often self-consciously assumed or performed and equally readily left off. The UK's Sarah Ratty, for instance, started out designing for 'New Age' travellers, and later in 1994–95 produced similar clothes for 'Conscious Earthwear', a fashion label for up market stores such as Browns and Harrods (de la Haye and Dingwell 1996). According to Eicher, ethnicity is a way of preserving an identity for groups of individuals, that links them to some meaningful heritage (Eicher 1995: 4). In traditional non-European cultures, this often was, and still is, expressed through dress, especially women's attire. But 'ethnic' dress as worn as a fashion or marker of the 'alternative' works differently. The appropriation of 'ethnic' style is itself uncritical and unspecific, suggesting wearers have general sympathy for oppressed minorities, rather than links to any specific known heritage or culture.

Alternative consumption

Although 'alternative' dressers reject the materialism of consumer culture, much of their clothing is embedded in that very culture and thus fully commodified. Alternative dress is composed of a mix of secondhand dress, low priced clothing bought at street or festival markets, often of Asian or South American origin, and extends to some custom or hand made items, such as beads, metal or thong necklaces and earrings, with hair specially braided and permanent or temporary tattoos. The market places themselves look similar around the world, taking their cue from the display or wares at street and rural markets in the under developed world (Figures 25 and 26). Hetherington suggests broadly two types of clothing assumed by 'New Age' travellers as part of the expression of identity, although one must caution against too prescriptive a categorisation. These types are what he terms the 'authentic' and those that can be associated with the tradition of the 'grotesque'. The first is often colourful and derived from Asian and romanticised gypsy style, and includes ethnic accessories, beads, talismans and Celtic design tattoos (Figures 24 and 26). One could add here inexpensive sandals, unstructured clothes, bracelets, braided hair and so on. The other, manifested by dirt and an unkempt appearance, can be merely a sign of the pragmatics of life on the road. More often it is a sign of resistance to western commodity culture, Green politics, anti-aesthetics or opposition to convention. Some travellers and 'crusties', he

25 Selling clothes, trinkets and food at the Djenne market, Mali 2003

suggests, use dirt as a cultivated form of image making and wear, for instance, old combat fatigues, have long matted dreadlock hair and body piercing (Hetherington 2000: 96). It is Hetherington's 'authentic' category of dress that is under discussion here.

In his theory of consumption written in the late nineteenth century, the sociologist Thorstein Veblen tried to explain fashion as something peculiar to the bourgeois classes, especially women. He used the notion of emulation as a way of explaining why fashion changes, suggesting they start with elite bourgeois women expressing their status with conspicuous expenditure on dress, wastefulness and endless novelty (Veblen 1934: 173). For Veblen it was also those who aspired to this class that emulated it. Once fashion is adopted by the lower classes, the elite are obliged to change their styles. A number of contemporary theorists have challenged this view, showing that fashion is no longer the preserve of a single elite group and therefore no longer works that way. Subcultures have effectively altered the landscape of dress as well. There are many cases where working-class or street fashion does not 'trickle down' from above but works in quite the reverse direction (Entwistle 2000: 62). Certain categories of Retro style, that is clothing which culls broadly from selected secondhand goods and disparate non-mainstream sources, have also entirely recon-figured the notion that style moves downwards. Angela McRobbie has

26 A young man with 'dreds', and a young woman with peasant style headscarf, selling jewellery and trinkets at Mullumbimby markets, New South Wales, 2002. Everyday jeans and T-shirts are worn by market customers at the rear

clearly shown, in her study of consumption and 'Retro' style in British cities, secondhand clothing is quite a distance from secondhand style. As she says, the 'subversive consumerism' of the rag market is in the practice of secondhand style, highly selective both in what it offers and also in what is purchased (McRobbie 1988: 29).

So where does 'New Age' dress fit into theoretical pictures of style? It is clearly not fashion or fad in the high street sense of the term. It is consciously chosen as a sign of belonging and as a sign of 'genuineness', apparently lacking in everyday dress. As a form of dress it purports to be the complete opposite of cosmopolitan, urban dress and thus can not quite be termed a fashion. Even so it has undergone changes over time, albeit small alterations, somewhat akin to fashion. Complicating the relationship between 'New Age' attire and everyday urban clothing is that alternative ideas about dressing, including the use of pre-used items, were rapidly co-opted as fashions by youth cultures and young professionals in the 1970s and 80s. Yet ironically for westerners who were forced by necessity to wear secondhand clothing in the 1980s, it still signalled shame and humiliation (Perry 1986: 39). It is the issue of choice that is the crucial factor.

Is Retro the same as 'alternative' clothing? Clearly both involve discriminating choices of secondhand style, self-consciously rummaging in

city markets for aesthetically appropriate items, as discussed by McRobbie
in her essay. But Retro is not 'New Age' style. The reason is that the latter
operates to some extent through individual choice, but the parameters of
this are fairly clearly established at the outset and there is a clearer
philosophy behind it. Although it should not be termed 'Retro' fashion
as such, the dress of those living, or purporting to live, an alternative life
has equally disturbed the links between class and consumption. It has
done so by attempting to displace fashion consumption in its strictest
sense, by using cheap, secondhand clothing and personally made or hand
crafted items. Some of this is part of a fundamental dislike of the hegemony
of the capitalist system itself but is also a protest against unnecessary
novelty and use of non-renewable resources. This is not to suggest that
'New Age' people are not consumers. Gifts, barter and money are all used
to exchange goods and services in the alternative life, although in recent
years their consumption practices have become more orthodox, only thinly
disguised as being pre-modern. They purchase secondhand clothing and
jewellery, have their bodies tattooed and faces painted, all for some return.
In an ironic twist of fate, mainstream society has found that there is
considerable commercial value in 'New Age' paraphernalia such as crystals,
tarot cards and aromatherapy, and the commodification of 'alternative' has
become extensive in both the high street and city mall.

Veblen longed for a utopian world where dress did not chase after the
novel but was beautiful and unchanging in its appearance, much like the
dress he imagined worn in traditional societies like China and Japan
(Veblen 1934: 176–7). In some ways alternative dressers who seek style
beyond everyday consumption, are just as romantic. Their message is that
the wearer has ethical commitment or some spiritual belief that is incom-
patible with modern progress, and out of tune with the crassness of mass
production. Yet the 'difference' of many 'New Age' lifestyle people is what
Clifford might term 'travelling-in-dwelling', for their way of living is only
possible as a counterpoint within the overarching safety of global commerce. There is also a more middle of the road and popular aspect to
'going back to nature', making your own clothing, eating 'natural foods'
and doing natural things with natural products reflected in books like, *The
Whole Earth Catalogue* and Alice Bay *Laurel's Living on the Earth. Living with
Natural Things*, first published in 1970. It also shows there are certain
aspirational linkage points between mainstream society and so called
alternative thinking.

To speak then of 'alternative' clothing is to concern oneself with
considerable levels of complexity. But there is little doubt that 'New Age'
and 'alternative' schemas and behavioural codes of dress are sufficiently
similar worldwide for us to be able to term them factors in a genuinely

global and generic alternative. It is a form of dressing that is both inside and outside the global framework. It is philosophically at odds with global consumption, and purports to be anti-materialistic and anti the western notion of capitalism. Yet at the same time it is still dependent on a worldwide marketing system for many items that are used by its practitioners. It is as if 'alternative' dressers occupy a second register of universal consumption. This is a way of dressing that impinges on the more obvious and dominating one at certain designated points of contact. But it is still unquestionably 'different'.

Notes

1 These photographs are in the 'Rainbow Archives', Mitchell Library, Sydney.

2 For a full coverage of the debate about terminology to time of publication, see Janice Newton (1988).

3 Nimbin, New South Wales, is still Australia's 'hippie' headquarters but it is now also a recommended tourist stop. The Nimbin Museum is regarded as an 'alternative museum' and houses a collection of Aquarius Festival memorabilia.

4 See www.inspiritdesigns.com/pages/InSpiritpages/bophotos.html (accessed July 2000), for photographs of a range of Rainbow family gatherings.

8 ✧ Clothing: is there a responsible choice?

In Inner Mongolia, in a village that lies between the Yellow River and the edge of the Gobi Desert Tian Shenhai lives ... in a house of sun-dried mud and straw, with a sand dune washed up against one of the walls. 'Twenty years ago the grass grew so high you couldn't see people' she said. (*Australian* 23 August 2001)

VISIT any major city shopping centre, mall, small town or weekend market in most parts of the world and you will almost certainly see crowds of people preoccupied with one of their favourite pastimes, shopping for clothes. In affluent countries it is primarily for new, or occasionally vintage clothes. In less prosperous countries it is more likely for secondhand garments, although there are of course many exceptions. Clothes lie at the centre of most economies, either as consumed articles or as goods produced. Some developing nations, Sri Lanka and Bangladesh for instance, actually depend for their livelihood on trading clothes and textiles. The consumption of textiles worldwide is remarkably extensive, with Germany and the US the highest per capita consumers.[1] The Fiber Economics Bureau reports that in 2000, 34.2 million metric tons of fibre were produced globally, with synthetics and polyester accounting for ninety four per cent of the total.[2] Reinforcing the picture of widespread consumption are statistics on recycling. In 1997 the USA Council for Textile Recycling recycled about 10 lbs of textiles each year for every person in the US. This computed to 1,250,000 tons, that is about a quarter of all post consumer waste.[3] Given the extent to which our world consumes clothing and textile products, we are faced with a number of dilemmas. Do we have the right to consume textiles at this level indefinitely, and at the same time ensure ecological sustainability? Can dressing continue to be a matter of personal or tactical choice, and also be part of the common good? Will the choice of what to wear for the vast majority, including ethnic differences, inevitably be subsumed into some form of featureless uniformity? Or will conventional textiles, clothing and their marketing be transformed in the

post-industrial age by new forms of visual communication, scientific dis-
coveries and computer technologies, such as computer-aided design and
manufacturing?[4]

Although production of apparel takes place in most parts of the world,
the degree of technological sophistication in manufacturing methods varies
widely, with most of the more developed nations having shifted production
off shore to Asia, the Philippines and even Eastern Europe. Dickerson
claims that the nature of apparel production is related to the stages of
industrial development reached by a country more generally. Once a
national economy becomes fully developed, she suggests, its apparel industry usually starts to have difficulty competing domestically. It then hives
off production to more profitable, low wage countries in the underdeveloped world (Dickerson 1999: 147). Although it is unwise to be
categorical when dealing with statistics, activities in apparel manufacturing
in 1996 certainly showed that combined textile and apparel production
in less developed countries accounted for more of total trade than that of
developed countries, and was continuing to grow (Dickerson 1999: 184).

Naomi Klein, in *No Logo* (2000), offers a particularly black view of
what is occurring in global production, including apparel making, in a
chapter entitled 'The Discarded Factory'. Here she argues that big global
companies, many based in the US, are shifting the responsibility of the
unattractive, polluting and even dangerous, side of manufacturing and
production off shore (Klein 2000: 201). These hugely profitable companies
act as content providers, concentrating on image and brand, but at the
same time deliberately disguise the precise details of where and how their
goods are made. So, in the developed world the industry may not be in
decline at all, but simply being repositioned. Competition, if we are to
believe Klein, is maintained extremely successfully, but at the expense of
factory or other production workers in poor countries. The environment
too pays a heavy price. One complicating factor is that in low wage
countries, employment in these factories may be the only source of income,
and to stop consuming may well do more harm than good. Another issue
is that the reach of e-markets has the potential to expand and extend the
sale of textiles and apparel, and may ultimately be of considerable advantage to the underdeveloped world. But the question remains, where does
the global dress consumer sit in moral and social terms, in any debate
about eco sustainability?

If we look beyond the marketing rhetoric and untroubled face of huge
corporations, scientific evidence shows much of the world's textile production and clothing maintenance is far from benign. It causes significant
amounts of pollution, and impacts heavily on ground water and soils
(Praveen *et al.* 1994). In fact all the fibres we use today, whether man-made

or otherwise, have some environmental impact. Leather and wool producing animals produce methane gas and denude grass lands, whilst cotton growing is an agricultural black spot. Although the degree of everyday clothing consumption seems to be stabilising (Lipovetsky 1994: 244), an increasingly politicised 'green' agenda in the west has engendered, amongst other things, a degree of moral concern about the damaging effects of textile production, and fears about unethical manufacturing practices.[5] This has contributed to what Lipovetsky terms a new ethical intensity in social democracies (Lipovestky 1994: 248–9). It often takes the form of a subtextual unease about global resource depletion and a matching concern for the world's ecosystems, especially amongst the young. An interesting issue is that eco sensitivity about clothing is not as intense as other concerns. So while many feel guilt about driving a car, express sympathy with oil spills and complain about yet more bulldozed forests, not so many realise the clothes they wear may derive from an equally significant environmental hazard. A one hundred per cent natural cotton shirt for example, unless organically grown without chemicals, is anything but 'natural'. It is a product nursed on pesticides, herbicides and defoliants. Its threads are likely to have been washed, softened, bleached, straightened and dyed – all processes that pollute (Kears 1992: 24).

However increased awareness of global environmental problems since the 1990s has engendered a number of targeted responses on the part of many manufacturers, and caused a shift in certain kinds of clothing consumption practices. In their chapter entitled 'Ecology', Gale and Kaur (2002) provide an excellent account of the place of textiles in 'green' debates, and chart the differing opinions about sustainable manufacturing practices, and the varied nature of governmental policies. One of the purposes of this chapter is to consider the extent to which environmental awareness has impacted on the policies of western clothing and apparel companies, flowing on to actual changes in patterns of consumption. Another intention is to think briefly about new scientific possibilities opening up for clothing design and its production.

There are a number of different manifestations of western eco concerns, as well as shifts in clothes buying, that are worth identifying if we are to give a comprehensive picture of dressing in both the developed and under developed world. These differences in attire lend further support to the theories outlined in chapter 1, that globalisation is made up of many uneven articulations of similarity and difference in style. But it must be acknowledged that ecological concerns are the privilege of the well off in our society, for the majority of global consumers do not have the kind of choice that can incorporate ethical considerations.

The growth of new categories of consumer in western economies, purportedly aware of environmental issues, has been quite marked in recent years. Wagner estimates that ten per cent of British consumers consistently integrate environmental issues into their buying behaviour (Wagner 1997: 2). Wagner also points out that 'green' consumers are not undifferentiated. They should instead be separated into various categories and degrees of commitment, with only a very small number, he believes, fully ideologically committed (Wagner 1997: 23). So running parallel to a western dominated middle market that consumes mass volume quite standardised clothing, are limited subsets of eco sensitive clothing.

Eco clothing looks similar to minimalist dress and appears equally functional and often comprised of leisure or informal wear. But it is different from mass styles in that it has purportedly been developed out of nostalgia for chemical-free, so called 'natural' fibres and pre-modern modes of production (Guerzioni and Troilo 1998: 174 and 176–8). Such attire is produced as a response to demands from 'green' consumers, seeking durable clothing, using fibres grown without environmental pollution. Guerzioni and Troilo argue that consumer desire to rediscover and then consume what they consider to be old style goods, in this instance so called pure or 'natural' garments, is part of the current 'hyper-differentiation' of consumption. It is also a form of dress, one could call a form of cultural capital, that subverts traditional desires for the 'newness' of new things, and the consumption of dress as luxurious (Guerzioni and Troilo 1998: 185 and 189). It has some particular elements in common with the consumption of 'authenticity', a feature of 'alternative' lifestyle purchases (see chapter 7).

A different subset, but in this case of mainstream, standardised clothing, with links to ecological clothing, is high performance outdoor sports wear. This is streamlined, functional, and ostensibly produced for consumers of extreme sports and adventure tourism. These clothes include the products of Rohan, the so-called 'adventure travel clothing company'. Rohan are committed to manufacturing protective, high security and all purpose wear of good quality. They have developed outer garments in what they call responsive 'Phase Change' fabrics that store and release heat, thus keeping the body at a constant temperature.[6] The company participates in a general discourse on environmentally appropriate dress and purports to be eco friendly, although this is debatable. In their commitment to practicality, Rohan clothing is not fashionable in the strict sense of the term, yet for those who can afford their expensive clothes they are regarded as a status symbol. In Bourdieu's terms it is dress used by the affluent or bourgeois class as a way of maintaining distinctiveness. It inferentially signals its presence by deliberate discretion and understatement (Bourdieu 1984: 249). So these quite highly priced, utilitarian clothes, with an aura of 'authenticity', are designed with specific purposes in mind. But for those who may not always use the clothing for its primary sportswear or travel functions, it is regarded in the same way as other relatively up market fashions.

Far more significant in terms of environmental sustainability is the purchasing and reuse of worn clothing, both in the developed world and in third world countries. For example, in the mid-1990s Wilderness Designs was one company taking fleece scraps from big companies including Patagonia and The North Face, and converting them into hats, mitts, socks and scarves with their product line called GARBage (Cole 1993: 1). Conversely, for populations in the less developed parts of the world, recycling of clothing is a necessity, and we have seen the important role it plays in places like India and Africa where huge volumes of secondhand goods have replaced or, to one degree or another, are interspersed with customary dress (Figure 27). In India, the sorting and sale of old clothes and rags or *chindi* is an integral part of the textile production industry, especially in places like Ahmedabad in the state of Gujarat, a centre for textile fabrication. Used clothing, orginally from the developed world, can also be part of a cycle of consumption that sees some of it returned to Europe and the US. Afghan refugees recycle secondhand western style sweaters, obtained through Pakistan, by unpicking them and knitting them up into slipper socks for sale back to the west (Herald 1992: 183). Occupying a further register of consumption is Retro, quality secondhand or vintage clothing, common to the developed world, and a stylish form of dressing that gestures to environmental sustainability yet remains outside the cycle of 'green' consumption.

It is interesting that the desire of affluent consumers to limit their consumption in some way, or participate in 'pure' or supposedly unsullied purchasing practices, has historical precedents. In the industrialised nineteenth century, facing somewhat similar momentous changes to society, people, like the utopian dress reformers, tried to distance themselves from current consumption patterns by wearing what they regarded as progressive, healthy or so called 'natural' attire (Wilson 1985: 210). Desire for 'authenticity' in dress and hairstyling continued to have currency, and came to drive some forms of 'alternative' attire. In her account of tensions in feminist thinking about fashion in the 1980s, Wilson discussed aspects of what she regarded as the still unresolved paradox between artifice and the 'natural'. She identified a debate between those who favour what she called ironic, modernist dress; clothing designed to deceive with its pleasurable, playful artificiality, and other kinds of feminist desires for 'authenticity' in clothing that were believed to be genuine and 'natural' (Wilson 1985: 230–1). One could suggest that this nature/culture divide, highlighted by Wilson, one evident between environmentally responsible clothing and

27 A Komakan village gathering in Mali, with the local headman in 1996. The women wear store-bought or secondhand clothes, and the woman in the centre has a locally made *chitenge* type flounced top, plus a customary, hand stitched indigo resist skirt

high catwalk fashion (and even some subcultural dress), still haunts
contemporary global dressing in the developed world. But the issue is
more complicated, for the 'natural' or 'authentic' has been commodified,
and drawn into the net of high fashion.[7] Elite consumption has plundered
the genuine styles of eco friendly wear for its own purposes.

Yet is the desire, and the decision to wear eco sensitive clothing, a
genuinely responsible one, or merely the whim of affluent or indeed 'New
Age' western consumers? And how prevalent is this kind of consumption?
Some purchasers, especially the young, resist mainstream clothing by buying
'green' or allegedly 'green' items such as hemp shoes, vegan Doc Martens
and Birkenstocks and Body Shop products. Yet the preference for recycled
clothing or environmentally friendly products exists within certain defined
parameters or repertoire of tastes, and can be a way of matching the style
of one's peers. It all hinges on differential notions of style or the current
framework of values, in which certain goods are deemed either socially
acceptable or inappropriate. Alfred Gell, in an essay dealing with consumption practices of the Muria Gonds in Central India, analyses their
particular values in which prestige, as signalled by choice of goods, is
sometimes shown by means of parsimony not wealth (Gell 1986: 111).
The Muria do not consume in the accepted western sense, rather they have
a desire to live up to a respectable, collective image that is non-competitive
and within the framework imposed by outsider Hindus. So their selection
and response to goods is neither natural nor value free, but operates in a
larger framework of values imposed by others (Gell 1986: 121).

So how much 'green' consumption is simply lip service and how much
genuine commitment? Is it possible, even desirable, in liberal democracies
that the attraction to fashionable novelty be dampened? Would not cutting
back on consumption eventually have a noticeable impact on the less
developed world, one that in fact depends on the importation and gifts
of used attire? Lipovetsky, a great advocate for social preoccupation with
trivial consumption, regards ecological consumption as much hedonistic
as any other and simply another marketing niche (Lipovetsky 1994: 248).
Some might regard this as overly cynical. Clearly, surrounding the consumption of 'green' or eco clothing are idealistic convictions of some kind,
although all point to a fragmentation or even a variety of subsets of dress
within the global marketplace.

The problems

From the 1970s onward, public and governmental concern about environmental depletion and pollution, especially in the developed countries,
became increasingly evident. Organisations such as Friends of the Earth

and Greenpeace were formed and we find the early use of the term 'recycling'. The first Greenpeace expedition to Amchitka nuclear test site, off the coast of Alaska, took place in 1971. The organisation began to gain worldwide attention over the following years. A new sense of urgency arose after the first UN General Assembly conference on the Human Environment in Stockholm in 1972, and publications like *Towards a Politics of Planet Earth* (1971) by Harold and Margaret Sprout and *The Limits to Growth* (1972), a report for The Club of Rome's project on the predicament of mankind. The latter contained warnings of the possible collapse of civilisation within a century, and raised important concerns about depletion of the world's resources. Other publications followed, including *The Global 2000 Report to the President: Entering the 21st Century* (1980). The general thrust of their content was to raise awareness of the strains of over population and consumption, depletion of resources, climate change, acid rain, destruction of tropical rainforests and global warming. The nature of concern changed in the 1980s to preoccupation with atmospheric pollution, so called 'forest death syndrome' and ozone depletion (Soroos 2000: 422–4). The UN Earth Summit conference in Rio de Janeiro in 1992, attended by more than 150 nations, sought a new concept of global inter-relatedness and co-operation on what was termed sustainable development. The Agenda 21 plan of action was agreed upon. A further Earth Summit was held in Johannesburg in 2002.

Since the mid-1990s consumer activists and the investigative media have increasingly drawn attention to the inequality between the US and other nations in terms of standards of living, levels of consumption and corresponding polluting practices. In 1995, one-fifth of the world's population, those living in the industrialised countries, were generating most of the toxic wastes, and were producing two-thirds of the greenhouse gases (Ophuls and Boyan 1995: 439). At the same time, awareness of the pollution caused by growing fibres like cotton, the problems of textile production processes and lack of enforceable codes of practice in the clothes manufacturing industry became the subject of increased political debate. Activists, anti-sweatshop lobbyists, anti-fur and anti-globalisation protesters began to expose some of the working conditions surrounding apparel production, especially in third world countries (Dickson 2001: 1).

Accessing reliable statistical information about levels of pollution caused by textile and even leather production is not easy. The companies in question are generally private enterprises who do not make this information public. Scientific estimates have been made, but even so it is hard to gauge the effects of these problems with any accuracy. Bahorsky quotes estimates that world textile pollutant chemicals numbered about 8,000 in 1998, and claims that up to fifty per cent of the world's pollution arises from fibre cultivation processing, and packaging into apparel (Bahorsky 1998: 691). Pollution occurs at every point of production, from cultivation, to processing, finishing and eventually at the level of washing or 'dry' cleaning. Some crops, especially cotton, take up a large proportion of the world's cultivated land. Other fibres like the polyesters are non-biodegradable. Toxic dyes and petroleum by-products are part of the manufacturing process of many textiles, with effluent draining into wells and rivers. Bleaching, moth proofing, domestic and industrial laundering and 'dry' cleaning causes further harm. Garments 'dry' cleaned are washed in hazardous substances that rely heavily on the chemical solvent perchloroethylene, used by an estimated eighty per cent of US dry cleaning establishments (Ryan 1996: 2). Moth proofing employs other dangerous substances, the synthetic pyrethroids. Tanning is another damaging finishing process, using chemicals like mineral salts, formaldehyde and coal-tar derivatives. Some statistics claim over 95 per cent of all leather tanned in the US is chrome tanned, with resulting hazardous effluent problems.[8]

While hemp is a fast growing crop that needs little fertilisers or pesticides, and is relatively eco friendly even when bleached, cotton is the reverse. It is one of the worst fibre offenders with little to recommend its manufacture or its long term use. It is a difficult and hazardous crop to grow and produce, yet in 1995 accounted for almost 50 per cent of the world's fibre production (Bahorsky 1998: 690). It is also a water greedy crop that depletes river systems and requires a huge use of fertilisers, pesticides and fungicides. One estimate puts a figure of 50 per cent of all insecticides used in third world countries are needed for growing cotton (Haggard 1990: 1). In Benin, West Africa the pesticide endosulfin used in cotton growing has caused many deaths among cotton workers (Abrams and Astill 2001: 3). The cotton fibre takes out nutrients from the soil and this in turn can eventually cause soil to degrade. In prosperous countries it is possible to let fields lie fallow but in the developing countries, cotton is a cash crop and this does not happen, which puts further strains on the land. For the most part cotton needs to be bleached in order to make it receptive to coloured dyes. Before weaving warp threads are covered with a surface dressing and the finished fabric treated with preservative, in some places of the pentochlorophenates type, which are very unsafe substances (Boudrup 1996: 11).

Ironically cotton has the reputation of being a 'natural' and healthy clothing fibre. It is the principle textile used to manufacture jeans, one of the world's most popular garments. Jeans are often regarded as working-class garments, thus democratic and 'authentic', and by extension ecologically friendly (Boudrup 1996: 12). They are produced in huge numbers over the world. One source estimated that in 1990 the British bought about

43 million pairs of jeans that year, nine out of ten of pure cotton (Haggard 1990: 1). This is a statistic based merely on one consuming country, clearly indicating the worldwide consumption of jeans is vast. It has been shown that Lee Cooper jeans, for instance, are made from cotton grown in West Africa using pesticides like endosulfin, and 'stone washed' with pumice. The latter is a damaging treatment that allows indigo dye to run off into streams, where it can kill plants and fish (Abrams and Astill 2001: 3). In other instances, blue denim can be an even bigger hazard, as it may be subjected to twelve separate dyeing or bleaching sessions to achieve just the right colour (Haggard 1990: 1). So to regard these garments as 'natural' is grossly erroneous. Yet what could be the alternative? If western consumers respond to the situation by boycotting cotton clothing, it will not necessarily remedy the situation. It is likely to have the same devastating effect as refusing to buy clothes made in the sweatshops of Vietnam, causing untold hardships to local growers and clothing workers. The ultimate irony is that jeans are a favoured item of dress for politically aware consumers, 'green' protesters and 'eco' sympathisers.

The changes

Corporate responses to ethical and environmental concerns and consumer pressure groups have been many and varied. The early 1990s was a period in which major clothing companies began to show signs of concern for the environment, many making pledges and ethical commitments, all integral to an emerging new phase of business practices. Over the next decade most significant textile companies were to develop corporate environmental policies (Gale and Kauer 2002: 117).[9] In 1999, responding to the shift toward 'green' purchasing in many European countries, the EU Eco-Label for textiles, set out its requirements and specific criteria for confirmation of clean processing and biodegradability. The 'No Sweatshop' lobby began to gain considerable momentum. Human rights, labour groups and student unions started to call for the establishment of responsible codes of practice in the apparel industries worldwide (*Business Week* May 3 1999).[10] The Fair Wear organisation was set up in Melbourne in 1996, to encourage retailers and manufacturers to support a code of conduct in the Textile, Clothing and Footwear industries, and help educate consumers about ethical shopping.

Changes have also occurred in agricultural practices. Since the late 1980s, some parts of the world, including the US and Denmark, have started organic cotton farming, in chemical free soil.[11] O Wear, established in 1992 and centred in Los Angeles, claims it is America's first 100 per cent certified organic cotton clothing company.[12] Organic cotton is also promoted by Nike, in its cotton based product range (Gale and Kaur 2002: 116). Yet, despite these developments, cotton fabrics are still routinely bleached and dyed, although naturally coloured cotton is grown by labels like Eco Logical fabrics and FoxFibre. The company Patagonia, who donates funds to environmental activism, still uses coloured dyes, which can cause even greater damage than agricultural chemicals (Broydo 1997: 1). Clearly the degree to which large corporations are willing to become 'green' is limited, and the extent to which these changes impact on the global consumption of unsustainably produced textiles and clothing is fairly minimal.

Some improvement to production practices have occurred as a direct result of protests by groups like PETA (People for the Ethical Treatment of Animals). For some years they have been conducting vigorous campaigns against the inhumane treatment of animals used to make clothing and footwear. PETA are strongly committed to direct action, offering guides to college activists and selling posters, stickers and sloganised T-shirts. Their website includes details of their anti-fur and anti-leather campaigns, such as the exposé of GAP who used Indian leather.[13] They also claim success with Reebok and Nike who have both pledged not to buy leather from Indian animals where basic animal protection laws are ignored. Much of their publicity is highly sensational, for instance the auction of Mary Tyler Moore's Russian Sable coat, which she donated to PETA, subsequently painted over in blood red paint with the words 'There's No Excuse. Fur Hurts'.[14] Although less noticeable since September 11 2001, this kind of extremism is an effective media draw card and matches the almost carnivalesque behaviour of anti-global protesters.

By 2003 many mainstream companies, especially manufacturers of leisurewear, catering to the younger market, eco tourists and outdoor sportswear, promoted themselves as responsible manufacturers. Numerous 'alternative' mail order companies and web marketing sites could supply consumers with eco friendly clothing, 'natural' and leather substitute products. For instance The Natural Collection catalogue from Greenpeace, with its organic cotton and hemp underwear, leisurewear, T-shirts and so on; Wearable Vegetables, Wildlife Works, People Tree, UK, a branch of the Japanese Fair Trade company in Tokyo and PETA's 'Cruelty Free' clothing, include Pleather, a textured faux leather made from PVC. Even so, it is unclear if these firms are as fully eco sensitive as they maintain. Since the 1990s many seem to have disappeared, are vague about their commitment to the environment, or remain small scale companies with limited customer outreach.[15]

As awareness grows of clothing and textiles as pollutants, many corporations are inventing new fibres and making changes to the ways fibres are processed, or have responded to ethical demands by using fully recycled materials. Tencel is the trade name for a man-made, cellulosic fibre called lyocell, made from tree pulp harvested from tree farms, not wilderness trees.[16] It is entirely recyclable and has the same properties as other cellulose derived materials like rayon, but with greater strength and softness (McLaren 1995: 38). Apparel made from recycled, post consumer PET drink bottles is a high grade polyester. Bailed and shredded bottles are remelted, extruded into a very soft cashmere-like fibre, then spun into new polyester material. According to McLaren, for every 3,700 two litre bottles recycled, one barrel of oil and ½ ton of toxic air emissions are saved (McLaren 1995: 39). Although it is hard to verify these statements, clearly using recycled material of any kind is an environmental plus. Yet it does not necessarily mean a major reduction in eco damage, and can simply have shifted or disguised the nature of the problem. Given the extent of consumption throughout the world, and huge population growth in places like China, these efforts remain merely gestures toward sustainability rather than any form of solution. All forms of clothing have some degree of environmental impact and to think that 'green' consumption could replace the current system is perhaps a misplaced one. The concept of corporate ethics is part of interlocking sets of responsibilities to the wider public concerning itself with stakeholders, employees, suppliers, producers and consumers, as well as with shareholders (Solomon 1991: 360–2). And there are supposed benefits for all in this kind of commitment. But are these policies just public relations exercises? Is a company that 'stands for something' really concerned in any way, or merely beating up its profits? After all there are billions of consumers of clothing in the world today, many of whom live on or below the poverty line, for whom 'green' issues are of no consequence and for whom charity clothing is the only option (Figure 28).

The customer

Running alongside the rhetoric of global eco sensitivity is a language engendered by large companies directed toward individuating shoppers and addressing the language of the local community (Humphrey 1998: 206). What TV and the internet has engendered is greater information about products and pricing, thus facilitating comparison shopping with increased selectivity. Sites like www.compare.com give consumers access to unbiased product review and the nature of relative, fluctuating costs. This has obliterated forever the notion of fixed prices and has placed the onus on the consumer with knowledge. But companies have also become sensitive to these new and more knowledgeable customers. It is they who are believed to desire social compassion and transparent ethical practices and priorities. More than ever the brand needs to persuade each and every customer that they are the company that cares in a general sense, but also for the customer in a particular sense. Alison Gill shows how brands like Nike create the appearance of belonging in a variety of ways, to create in consumers the sense of security, meaning and identity, as real as belonging to an actual place or family (Gill 2000: 95)

28 Charity clothing worn by a group of Bambara children in Mali, 1996. The mother standing behind is dressed in a local print dress

In some cases this purported company caring can be a dramatic gesturing toward world problems as with Benetton, or a more kindly rhetoric, that focuses on the company's social concern and charitable activities (charity of course has been fashion's long time associate). Part of the effectiveness of a brand is its capacity to embody a 'point of view', something that in turn makes it simpler to sell to busy customers. A 'point of view' can be a collection of marketing positions about a product, but it can also embody ancillary charitable activities, educational projects or supposed social compassion, as is the case with Nike and Benetton. This rhetoric includes commitment to socially responsible labour codes of practice, and a supposed sensitivity to the needs and tastes of the customer. In some especially fascinating ways, compassion and personal attention are folded into the marketing strategies of branded goods and clothing lines, and used to further enhance a company's reputation. Dickerson claims part of the success of Levi Strauss, besides the popular cultural trend for jeans wearing, is its rhetoric claiming to be culturally sensitive and socially responsible marketer (Dickerson 1999: 445).[17] The emotive words 'empathy–originality–integrity–courage' as core company values are emblazoned at the top of their homepage www.levistrauss.com.

Benetton, in fact, has set itself up as a form of corporate voice for public morality and social justice. This was especially evident in the sensational 'social realist' Toscani advertisements it began to use from 1991 (Giroux 1993–94: 9), in particular the 'Shock of Reality' campaign of 1992. As Giroux argues, these dramatic images in which there was an absence of product, were also skilfully manipulated to decontextualise them from their political realities and associated facts. They were then reframed as commerce by the addition of the company logo. Here Benetton offered a problematic transgression of cultural categories, by the drawing together of two symbolically different sign systems, the 'real' world of the documentary and the superficial world of fashion (Antick 2002: 93). Despite official company denials that the images were intended expressly for commercial gain, their sensationalism, and the ensuing debate, produced outstanding media coverage and hence company profits. All this changed in January 2000 when Benetton ran the 'We On Death Row' campaign, showing prisoners on death row in the US. This went too far for Benetton's US franchise partners, Sears, Roebuck and Co. They no longer regarded the company as socially responsible and pulled out of the arrangement (Ehrenreich 2000: 20), causing a serious downturn in the fortunes of Benetton at that time.

Nike is another good example of the projection of compassion and philanthropy, supposedly fighting racial bias with community aid, and promoting Nike at the same time. Some of their softer rhetoric seems to have been a response to customer anger at company production methods and is perhaps one of the outcomes of the big anti-Nike protests against labour practices from the late 1990s. Examples of their efforts include the Nike PLAY program to sponsor inner city sports programs, and the building of Habitat for Humanity House, for a low income family in Portland, the headquarters of the company. In 2001, one thousand Nike employees, friends and families took part in a human relations exercise and fundraiser, the 'Walk As One' event, wearing 'We are Nike' T-shirts, showing support for community, diversity and family. Benetton has set up similar projects, including a Museum in Patagonia. But the brand never suffers, for all publicity is ultimately good publicity.

Multi-nationals have certainly come to regard ethical responsibility and compassion as a high priority. Even so, whilst from the late 1990s they rushed to establish voluntary codes of company conduct, there is still no universal standard of ethical behaviour for global corporations (Klein 2000: 434). This suggests a careful calculation on the part of companies cashing in on compassion, but with a less than total commitment to maintaining community standards and ethical practices. Many companies are engaged in active research and development programmes, and the subtext of their so called ethical responsibility may be a desire to find alternatives to traditional methods of growing and processing fibres.

Clothing and the new technology

Some of the most intriguing developments in dress in recent years have been the development of high performance fabrics and electronic clothing. Sometimes called 'Smart' or intelligent clothes, these are garments designed with an integrated mixture of electronic and new textile technology, that is 'Smart' fibres and techno textiles. Fabrics, with multi-functional and trans-seasonal performance capabilities, are used to make garments that incorporate personal computers. These high tech, test tube textiles are functional, lightweight and adaptable. Some companies are even experimenting with mood altering garments, and clothing that fits like a second skin, actually growing and regenerating as you wear it, with seams expanding to accommodate changes in weight (Hamilton and Martineau 1997: 1). Others like DuPont have developed CoolMax, a fabric that regulates body temperature. This is a revolutionary development toward consumer empowerment, allowing personal control of the micro environment, the capacity to monitor ones health, and satisfy personal communication needs. Such dress is less about fashion in the old sense, and more about lifestyle, utility and all purposefulness.

Media Lab at MIT was the first group to experiment with wearable computing and the MIThril Wearable Computing website details current projects and the latest thinking on wearable electronics.[18] Other companies like Philips have taken a more consumer conscious approach. The aim for Philips, and a number of companies who research and develop new, marketable forms of clothing, the PE Group (Personal Electronics) for instance, has been to create clothing that is a self-contained resource and transmitting centre, allowing maximum freedom and the ability to communicate effectively with others. Functional in appearance, this clothing has moved some distance from the utopian dress reform ideas of the past and the idealistic clothes of proponents of environmental sustainability, yet in another sense it is both futuristic and utilitarian in the truest sense of the word.

In fact in the mid-1990s Philips electronics began exploring the field of electronic fashion, as way of looking to the future of clothing. They produced their *Wearable Electronics* collection in 1999 and *New Nomads* in 2000. This latter collection was designed for professional people, for sports enthusiasts, for children, and as street and club wear for young people (Philips Design 2000: 22). In August 2000 Philips, in partnership with Levi Strauss, advertised branded Industrial Clothing called ICD+ which consisted of four different networked jackets containing a body area network for practical daily use.[19] Designed by Massimo Osti, this was an entirely new concept in clothing that intended to help people communicate and achieve greater sense of personal freedom by fusing technology with clothing.[20] Most of Philips products are based on a Personal Area Network or PAN, which provides a backbone for wearable electronics, allowing the consumer to decide on what functionality they needed to meet the day's requirements.

Philips intended these clothes to provide personal information, assist in knowing the immediate environment and help the wearer to react intelligently. Modular devices could be hooked up to the network, allowing interaction with the invisible collar microphones, mobile phone audio player, miniature cameras and temperature sensors. They were designed as 'an adaptable solution' for a typical nomadic consumer who worked in a modern city, and wanted to keep their day to day electronics near at hand. Some had fabrics that were sensuous and mood enhancing. They conditioned or massaged the skin, responded to the temperature of the surrounding environment and warmed one up or cooled one down as desired. So Philips 'New Nomads' products are a synergic merger of technology and fashion, the aim according to the company, to free the wearer, making them both omnipotent and omnipresent.[21] This technological and sensory capability must surely be the ultimate form of customisation that clothing can achieve. Interestingly Philips have managed to fit 'smart' clothing into the rhetoric of both a caring company and an environmentally sensitive one. They argue that technology is a fundamental aspect that helps nurture our physical and mental wellbeing, and that communication technology saves consumption and therefore has less impact on the environment (Philips Design 2000: 12–13).

At this point it is important to consider what might be clothing's long term future. If the fundamental tenet upon which fashion operates is endless novelty and change, one might say that the very basis of 'new' fashions is a harmful practice. For some consumers, distaste for fashion's changes has brought about a form of moral desire to reject the styles of the mall, for what they regard as a superior form of unsullied consumption. In western culture particularly, we find this curious paradox; the desire to purchase but not to consume pointlessly, rather in a sober, responsible, even utilitarian manner. Responsible apparel consumption, as a concept, matches in part consumer desires for organic food, ecologically sustainable domestic appliances and even eco travel. The choice of attire may include the streamlined efficient wear of companies like Rohan, or organically sound products made according to 'green' principles, and might include the purchasing of Retro or secondhand clothes, although these three categories are not necessarily related. Some of this new mood has manifested itself in the taste for minimalist clothing, the reverse of the conspicuous consumption of the 1980s, and relates to the ways in which sports clothing has led design ideas for everyday dress. It is also linked to the current push to develop technologically new fabrics for high performance and extreme sports, like Nike's FIT (functional, innovative, technology apparel), as well as the design of so called 'smart' textiles and garments, although 'smart' clothes are not necessarily friendly to the environment and may prove to be extremely difficult to maintain.

All of this fails to appreciate the significant part that continues to be played by western secondhand dress in the less developed areas of the globe like Africa and India. But these alternatives do raise the important issue of what might constitute ethically responsible dressing, for a world stressed and strained by environmental problems. In the final analysis, will the choice of what to wear inevitably be subsumed into some form of functionality or high tech 'smart' attire? New technologies purport to be the way of the future in dress capitalising on utility and simplicity. But the fundamental basis on which global capitalism works, is centred on the consumption of new things. If we go down the track of utilitarian dress, we might deny work opportunities to millions, especially in underdeveloped nations. We also deny self-identity, as well as ethical and national distinctions, and thus a degree of self-empowerment. As we have seen, even when faced with only secondhand goods to wear, consumers in the under developed world still exert a degree of choice and self-selection. If in the end consumers have the economic power to purchase 'smart' or technologically advanced forms of clothing, then fashion will play its part and these garments are likely to be as resource hungry as any other forms of clothing. But it is difficult seriously to imagine that technological clothing will become global clothing in any real sense. Within the parameters of affordability, the vast majority of people in the world will continue to wear clothing for comfort, social, cultural and psychological ease, to communicate with others, and of course simply to protect themselves from the elements.

Notes

1 Eberle, 'Towards sustainability in the textile clothing chain', www.oeko.de/bereiche/produkte/sustex.html, accessed November 2001.

2 www.fibersource.com/f-info/fiber%20production.htm, accessed October 2001.

3 www.textilerecycle.org/, accessed November 2001. These statistics are tempered somewhat by the fact that about 48 per cent of post consumer textile waste in the US is recycled as secondhand clothing, and sold on to underdeveloped countries. The Council claimed that in 1989 the annual per capita consumption of fibre in the US was 67.9 lbs.

4 Gale and Kaur discuss and speculate about the impact of the internet, and e-markets, on the global textile industry and its trading networks (2002: 130–2).

5 On the other hand the higher fashion retail market was buoyant in the 1990s, growing from 16 billion in 1992, to 24 billion in 1998. See Moore *et al*. 2000: 12.

6 www.rohan.co.uk/, accessed November 2001.

7 For an account of the 'authenticity' debate that has centred on the supposed 'natural' hairstyling of both black and white customers, see Cox (1999: 264).

8 http://unreasonable.org/vegan/leather-substitutes.html, 20 April 2000, accessed August 2000.

9 Rather unusually Ermenegildo Zegna, manufacturer of high quality textiles and menswear, has been involved in environmental education, sustenance of the wilderness, forest reserving and conservation for over 60 years (*The Economist*, 2000: 1).

10 A 'No Sweat Shop' label was launched in Australia in 2001 but has not been overwhelmingly supported.

11 Denmark was the first country to manufacture ecological cotton and make it a profitable enterprise (Boudrup 1996: 13).

12 http://iisd.ca/business/owear.htm, accessed November 2001. They won the first United Nations Environment Programme's 'Fashion and the Environment' Award in 1993.

13 www.peta-online.org/ with links to www.cowsarecool.com. More information and news releases can be found on the 'Fur is Dead' website www.furisdead.com, accessed November 2001.

14 www.allstarcharity.com/lot00598.html, accessed November 2001.

15 In the 1990s, Vaude developed a fully recyclable Ecolog collection. Everything in the garments, from buttons and zippers, to fabric and fleece, was made of polyester. Used garments, returned to distributors were guaranteed to be ground up, shredded or melted into a granulate to become buttons, zippers or other products (Cole 1993: 1). But in 2001 the company, now called Vaude Sports Ltd, seemed to have a somewhat less committed attitude to the environment.

16 www.tencel.com/, accessed October 2001.

17 Levi Strauss was the first company to develop an ethical code of conduct for its workers.

18 http://agents.www.media.mit.edu/projects/wearables, accessed November 2001.

19 www.research.philips.com/pressmedia/releases/000801.html, accessed November 2001.

20 www.research.philips.com/pressmedia/releases/990802.html, accessed November 2001.

21 www.design.philips.com/smartconnections/newnomads/index.html, accessed November 2001.

Conclusion

THROUGHOUT the history of dress, clothing has been used as an important indicator of personal, religious and group affiliations, as well as to denote social hierarchies and power relationships. It has been one of the primary and most immediately visible markers of differential cultural practices. These capabilities for clothing differ little for societies in the twenty-first century. But what is different is a rhetoric that claims we occupy an increasingly homogenous world, and that the subtleties of traditional dress and textiles are less evident, and therefore less meaningful. No one can deny that new forms of electronic communication, shared understandings and international business practices, and indeed the practical requirements of contemporary life, continue to influence people in many different parts of the world in their selection of clothing. Many do make very similar choices, and for very similar reasons. Fashion is one, but there are also economic imperatives, wearing qualities and suitability, and some for quite different reasons relating to culture, group cohesion, resistance and the political. But regardless of the tendency toward similarity of attire, dress within the global context should certainly not be regarded in any way as uniform.

Eicher, in her important texts *Dress and Ethnicity* and *The Visible Self* coined the term 'world dress' for this commonly worn clothing. But the present project has probed beyond the generalisation of the term 'world dress', and examined the notion of homogeneity a little more closely. In doing so it has shown that we need a fuller, more nuanced understanding of the complications inherent in so called global style. It demonstrates that dress styles are relational, often tactical, and, where economic level permits, their assumption is based on careful choice and very considered selection. People who do assume international clothing of one sort or another, business suits, jeans, baseball caps and the like, and those who dress in local attire, be it 'ethnic', regional, national or customary, are all engaged in multifarious style accommodations and resistances, in their day-to-day choices of self-presentation. It has been shown that global consumers of western style apparel, as well as those who practice 'alternative' forms of consumption, are acculturated through the use of clothing.

To gain a comprehensive understanding of such selective 'wearing', this investigation includes a study not only of higher social and professional echelons, but those who live at the social margins and those whose access to new clothes is necessarily minimal. Even with the latter, dress is hardly a matter of uniformity or discrete meanings. Rather it is the case that in the decisions people make about their attire, even of the most limited kinds, conformity to global style is only part of the consideration. Multifarious factors enter into choice of apparel, some more significant than others. For many, adoption of western clothing may well be an overriding one as the tentacles of global propaganda reach into every corner of the world and what is increasingly evident is that western clothing provides the most versatile options for consumers. But these options are not always accepted wholeheartedly, and may be overridden by other considerations.

In no part of the world do we see fully homogenised dressing, that is everybody entirely dressed in western fashions, for all societies are made up of different income levels, professions and affiliations. Instead there are complicated disjunctures between similarity and difference, played out on a day-to-day basis. And the meanings of dress do not speak simply to a single audience; they are variously decoded as you move from one culture to the next. Yet the concept of creolisation or hybridity in dress is only a part of the picture. A more realistic view of what is happening is that global dress is an uneven montage of differing tastes and imperatives. People who live in Mauritania, Mongolia and New York may well wear jeans and T-shirts that appear to be exactly the same, but others in those same places may be wearing clothes linked to their own cultures, or borrowed in part, or even wholly from that of others. Everywhere we look, people who live in cities, as well as those who work in and inhabit rural environments, are engaged in tactical decisions about what to wear, formulating their appearances in careful and considered ways.

Perhaps one could offer the hypothesis that if there is such a concept as truly globalised clothing, it is not necessarily entirely western in origin. Rather it is a patchwork of many different styles in which the international plays a dominant role. And if there is to be a global attire that endures for the future, perhaps it will continue be an amalgam of designs, ideals and aspirations, dress that is both culturally circumscribed but also clothing that transcends geographical boundaries.

Bibliography

Books and articles

Abrams, F. and J. Astill (2001) 'Story of the blues', *Guardian*, 29 June, G2 1–4.

Abu-Lughod, L. (1990) 'The romances of resistance: tracing transformations of power through Bedouin women', *American Ethnologist*, 17, 41–55.

Antick, P. (2002) 'Bloody jumpers: Benetton and the mechanics of cultural exclusion', *Fashion Theory*, 6: 1, 83–109.

Appadurai, A. (ed.) (1986) *The Social Life of Things: Commodities in Cultural Perspective*, Cambridge: Cambridge University Press.

—— (1996) *Modernity at Large: Cultural Dimensions of Globalisation*, Minneapolis: University of Minnesota Press.

Bahorsky, M. S. (1998) 'Textiles: regulatory aspects and reviews', *Water Environment Research*, 70:4, 690–3.

Ballinger, J. (2001) 'Nike's voice looms large', *Social Policy*, 32, 34–8.

Barnard, M. (1996) *Fashion as Communication*, New York: Routledge.

Barthes, R. (1983) *The Fashion System*, New York: Hill and Wang.

Bastian, M. L. (1996) 'Female *"alharjis"* and entrepreneurial fashions: flexible identities in Southeastern Nigerian clothing practice', in *Clothing and Difference: Embodied Identities in Colonial and Post-Colonial Africa*, ed. H. Hendrickson, Durham: Duke University Press, 97–132.

Baudrillard, J. (1981) 'Sign function and class logic', in *For a Critique of the Political Economy of the Sign*, trans. C. Levin, St Louis: Telos Press.

Bell, J. (2001) '"New world order" a review of *No Logo* by Naomi Klein', *Things*, 14 Summer, 90–6.

Benstock, S. and S. Ferriss (eds.) (1994) 'Introduction', in *On Fashion*, New Brunswick: Rutgers University Press, 1–17.

Berry, S. (2000) 'Be our brand: fashion and personalisation on the web', in *Fashion Cultures: Theories, Explorations and Analysis*, eds. S. Bruzzi and P. Church Gibson, London: Routledge, 49–60.

Biaya, T. K. (1998) 'Hair statements in urban Africa', in *The Art of African Fashion*, eds. E. van der Plas and M. Willemsen, Eritrea: Africa World Press.

Blau, H. (1999) *Nothing of Itself: Complexions of Fashion*, Bloomington: Indiana University Press.

Boudrup, J. (1996) 'Textile materials and ecology. Part one', *Newsletter of the Guild of Danish Weavers and Printers*, No. 1, trans. K. Finch, 2001.

Boultwood A. and R. Jerrard (2000) 'Ambivalence, and its relation to fashion and the body', *Fashion Theory*, 4:3, 301–22.

Bourdieu, P. (1984) *Distinction: A Social Critique of the Judgement of Taste*, trans. R. Nice, Cambridge Massachusetts: Harvard University Press.

Breu, M. and R. Marchese (2000) 'Social commentary and political action: the headscarf as popular culture and symbol of political confrontation in modern Turkey', *Journal of Popular Culture*, 33:4 Spring, 25–38.

Breward, C. (1995) *The Culture of Fashion: A New History of Fashionable Dress*, Manchester: Manchester University Press.

—— (1998) 'Cultures, identities, histories: fashioning a cultural approach to dress', *Fashion Theory*, 2:4, 301–14.

Bridgeman, J. (2000) ' "Pagare le pompe". Why Quattrocentro sumptuary laws did not work', in *Women in Italian Renaissance Culture and Society*, ed. L. Panizza, Oxford: Legenda, 209–26.

Brodman, B. (1994) 'Paris or perish: the plight of the Latin American Indian in a westernized world', in *On Fashion*, eds. S. Benstock and S. Ferriss, Brunswick New Jersey: Rutgers University Press, 267–83.

Broydo, L. (1997) 'Clothing argument: for duds that don't wear on the planet, the best bet is to buy used,' *Mother Jones*, 22:4 July–August InfoTrac.

Campbell, C. (1997) 'When the meaning is not a message: a critique of the consumption as communication thesis', in *Buy This Book: Studies in Advertising and Consumption*, eds. M. Nava, A. Blake, I. Macrury and B. Richards, London: Routledge, 340–51.

Camuffo, A. P. Romano and A. Vinelli (2001), 'Back to the future: Benetton transforms its global network', *MIT Sloan Management Review*, 43 Fall, 46–52.

Childs P. and R. J. Williams (1997) *Introduction to Post-Colonial Theory*, London: Prentice-Hall.

Clark, H. (1999) 'The cheungsam: issues of fashion and cultural identity', in *China Chic: East meets West*, eds. V. Steele and J. S. Major, New Haven: Yale University Press, 155–65.

—— (2000) 'Fashion, identity and the city: Hong Kong', *Form/Work*, 4, 81–92.

Clarke, J., S. Hall, T. Jefferson, and B. Roberts (1981) 'Sub cultures, cultures and class', in *Culture, Ideology and Social Process*, eds. T. Bennett, G. Martin, C. Mercer, J. Woollacott, London: Batsford Academic and Educational Ltd. In association with The Open University Press, 53–79.

Clifford, J. (1992) 'Travelling Cultures', in *Cultural Studies*, eds. L. Grossberg, C. Nelson and P. A. Treichler, New York: Routledge, 96–116.

Cock, P. (1979) *Alternative Australia*, Melbourne: Quarter Books.

Cocks, J. (1988) 'Scarves and Minds', *Time*, 131 21 March, InfoTrac.

Cole, M. (1993) 'Talking about eco-lution', *Women's Sports and Fitness*, 15:8 December. InfoTrac.

Comaroff, J. and J. (1992) *Ethnography and the Historical Imagination*, Boulder Colorado: West View Press.

Cox, C. (1999) *Good Hair Days. A History of British Hairdressing*, London: Quartet Books.

Craig, M. (1997) 'The decline and fall of the conk; or, how to read a process', *Fashion Theory*, 1:4, 399–420.

Craik, J. (1994) *The Face of Fashion. Cultural Studies in Fashion*, London: Routledge.

Crane, D. (2000) *Fashion and its Social Agendas: Class, Gender and Identity in Clothing*, Chicago: University of Chicago Press.

Crewe, L. and A. Goodrum (2000) 'Fashioning new forms of consumption: the case of Paul Smith', in *Fashion Cultures: Theories, Explorations and Analysis*, eds. S. Bruzzi and P. Church Gibson, London: Routledge, 25–48.

Crewe, L. and M. Lowe (1996) 'United colours? Globalisation and localisation tendencies in fashion retailing', in *Retailing Consumption and Capital*, eds. N. Wrigley and M. Lowe, Harlow: Longman, 271–83.

Cunningham, C. E. (1998) 'The interaction of cultural performances, tourism and ethnicity', *Journal of Musicological Research*, 17:2, 81–5.

Dalby, L. (1993) *Kimono: Fashioning Culture*, New Haven: Yale University Press.

Danandjaja, J. (1997) 'From hansop to safari: notes from an eyewitness', in *Outward Appearances: Dressing State and Society in Indonesia*, ed. H. S. Nordholt, Leiden: KITVL Press, 249–58.

Dant, T. (1999) *Material Culture in the Social World*, Buckingham: Open University Press.

Davis, F. (1992) *Fashion, Culture and Identity*, Chicago: Chicago University Press.

De Certeau, M. (1984) *The Practice of Everyday Life*, Berkeley: University of California Press.

de la Haye, A. and C. Dingwell (1996) *Surfers Soulies Skinheads and Skaters: Subcultural Style from the Forties to the Nineties*, London: Victoria and Albert Museum.

Derrida, J. (1998) *Limited Inc.*, Evanston: Northwestern University.

Dickerson, K. G. (1999) *Textiles and Apparel in the Global Economy*, Upper Saddle River New Jersey: Merrill.

Dickson, M. A. (2001) 'Utility of no sweat labels for apparel consumers', *Journal of Consumer Affairs*, 35 Summer. InfoTrac.

Driver, S. and L. Martell (1999) 'New Labour: culture and economy', in *Culture and Economy After the Cultural Turn*, London: Sage, 246–69.

du Gay, P., S. Hall, L. James, H. Mackay and K. Negus (1997) *Doing Cultural Studies: The Story of the Sony Walkman*, London: Sage.

Durham, D. (1999) 'The predicament of dress: polyvalency and the ironies of cultural identity', *American Ethnologist* 26:2, 389–411.

Dwyer, C. (1999) 'Veiled meanings: young British Muslim women and the negotiation of differences', *Gender, Place and Culture*, 6:1, 5–26.

Eberle, U. (1998) 'Towards sustainability in the textile clothing chain', www.oeko.de/bereiche/produkte/sustex.html, (accessed November 2001) Eurotex Bulletin 1, 2000.

Ehrenreich, B. (2000) 'Dirty laundry: Benettons "We On Death Row" campaign', *Aperture*, 160 Summer, 20–5.

Eicher, J. B. (ed.) (1995) *Dress and Ethnicity: Change Across Space and Time*, Oxford: Berg.

—— and B. Sumberg (1995) 'World fashion, ethnic and national dress', in *Dress and Ethnicity: Change Across Space and Time*, ed. J. B. Eicher, Oxford: Berg, 295–306.

—— S. L. Evenson and Lutz, H. A. (2000) *The Visible Self: Global Perspectives on Dress, Culture, and Society*, second edn, New York: Fairchild.

El Guindi, F. (1999) *Veil, Modesty, Privacy and Resistance*, Oxford: Berg.

Eller, J. (1997) 'Ethnicity culture and the past', *Michigan Quarterly Review*, 36 Fall, 552–600.

Entwistle, J. (1997) '"Power dressing" and the construction of the career woman', in *Buy This Book: Studies in Advertising and Consumption*, eds. M. Nava, A. Blake, I. Macrury and B. Richards, London: Routledge, 311–23.

—— (2000a) *The Fashioned Body: Fashion Dress and Modern Social Theory*, Cambridge: Polity Press.

—— (2000b) 'Fashioning the career woman: power dressing as a strategy of consumption', in *All the World and her Husband: Woman in Twentieth Century Consumer Culture*, eds. M. Andrews and M. Talbot, London: Cassell, 224–38.

Evans, C. (1997) 'Dreams that only money can buy … or the shy tribe in flight from discourse', *Fashion Theory*, 1:2, 169–88.

Everard, J. (1999) 'Crossing cultures in cyberspaces; navigating realities between the "real" and the "virtual"', in *Impossible Selves: Cultural Readings of Identity*, eds. J. Lo, D. Beard, R. Cunneen and D. Ganguly, Melbourne: Australian Scholarly Publishing.

Fandy, M. (1998) 'Political science without clothes: the politics of dress or contesting the spatiality of the state in Egypt', *Arab Studies Quarterly*, 20:2 Spring. InfoTrac.

Franklin, A. (2001) 'Black women and self-presentation: appearing in (dis)guise', in *Through the Wardrobe: Women's Relationships with their Clothes*, eds. A. Guy, E. Green, M. Banim, Oxford: Berg, 137–150.

Friedman, J. (1994) *Cultural Identity and Global Process*, London: Sage.

—— (1998) 'Knowing Oceania or Oceania knowing: identifying actors and activating identities in turbulent times', in *Pacific Answers to Western Hegemony: Cultural Practices of Identity Construction*, ed. J. Wassmann, Oxford: Berg, 37–66.

Gale, C. and J. Kaur (2002) *The Textile Book*, Oxford: Berg.

Gell, A. (1986) 'Newcomers to the world of goods: consumption among the Muria Gonds', *The Social Life of Things: Commodities in Cultural Perspective*, ed. A. Appadurai, Cambridge: Cambridge University Press, 110–38.

Gilbert, D. (2000) 'Urban outfitting: the city and the spaces of fashion culture' *Fashion Cultures: Theories, Explorations and Analysis*, eds. S. Bruzzi and P. Church Gibson, London: Routledge, 7–24.

Gill, A. (2000) 'Belonging with the Swoosh: On cyborg clothing and part-objects', *Form/Work*, 4 March, 93–128.

Giroux, H. A. (1993–94) 'Consuming social change: the united colours of Benetton', *Cultural Critique*, 26 Winter 5–32.

Goldman, D. S. (1997) '"Down for La Raza": Barrio art t-shirts, Chicano pride, and cultural resistance', *Journal of Folklore Research*, 34:2, 123–38.

Goldstein-Gidoni, O. (1999) 'Kimono and the construction of gendered and cultural identities' *Ethnology*, 38:4 Fall. InfoTrac.

Guerzoni, G. and G. Troilo (1998) 'Mass rarefaction of consumption and the emerging consumer-collector', in *The Active Consumer: Novelty and Surprise in Consumer Choice*, ed. M. Bianchi, London: Routledge.

Haggard, C. (1990) 'Green Jeans', *The Economist Annual*. InfoTrac.

Hansen, K. T. (1994) 'Dealing with used clothing: *salaula* and the construction of identity in Zambia's third republic', *Public Culture*, 6:3 Spring, 503–23.

—— (1995) 'Transnational biographies and local meanings: used clothing practices in Lusaka' in J. B. Eicher, S. L. Evenson, H. A. Lutz, *The Visible Self: Global Perspectives on Dress, Culture and Society*, second edn, New York: Fairchild, 2000, 277–284.

—— (1999) 'Second-hand clothing encounters in Zambia: global discourses, western commodities, and local histories', *Africa*, 69 Summer. InfoTrac.

—— (2000) 'Other people's clothes? The international second-hand clothing trade and dress practices in Zambia', *Fashion Theory*, 4:3, 245–74.

Hassan, S. M. (1998) 'Henna mania: body painting as a fashion statement from tradition to Madonna', in *The Art of African Fashion*, eds. E. van der Plas and M. Willemsen, Eritrea: Africa World Press.

Hendrickson, H. (ed.) (1996) *Clothing and Difference. Embodied Identities in Colonial and Post-Colonial Africa*, Durham: Duke University Press.

Hepburn, S. (2000) 'The cloth of barbaric pagans: tourism, identity and modernity in Nepal', *Fashion Theory*, 4:3, 275–300.

Herald, J. (1992) *World Crafts*, London: Charles Letts and Co.

Hetherington, K. (2000) *New Age Travellers*, London: Cassell.

Hiltebeitel, A. (1998) 'Introduction: hair tropes', in *Hair: Its Power and Meaning in Asian Cultures*, eds. A. Hiltebeitel and B. D. Miller, Albany: State University of New York Press.

Hiwasaki, L. (2000) 'Ethnic tourism in Hokkaido and the shaping of Ainu identity', *Pacific Affairs*, 73:3, 393–412.

Hollander, A. (1980) *Seeing Through Clothes*, New York: Avon Books.

—— (1993) 'Accounting for fashion', *Raritan*, 13:2, 121–32.

—— (1995) *Sex and Suits*, New York: Kodansha International.

Holton, R. (1998) 'Globalisation and Australian identities', in *Australian Identities*, ed. D. Day, Melbourne: Australian Scholarly Publishing, 198–211.

Houston, J. (1996) *A Mythic Life: Learning to Live our Greator Story*, San Francisco: Harper.

Howes, D. (1996) *Cross Cultural Consumption: Global Markets, Local Realities*, London: Routledge.

Hoy, J. (2000) 'The Americanisation of the outback: cowboys and stockmen', *Journal of Australian Studies*, 66, 205–10.

Humphrey, K. (1998) *Self-Life: Supermarkets and the Changing Cultures of Consumption*, Melbourne: Cambridge University Press.

Jameson, F. (1999) 'Notes on globalization as philosophical issue', in *The Cultures of Globalization*, eds. F. Jameson and M. Miyoshi, Durham: Duke University Press, 54–77.

Jenkins, R. (1997) *Rethinking Ethnicity: Arguments and Explorations*, London: Sage.

Jiggens, J. (1983) *Rehearsals for the Apocalypse*, Brisbane: Tuntable Falls Network Publishing.

Johnson, R. (1994) 'Dressed to acquit', *Allure*, December, 98 and 107–10.

Johnson, V. (1996) *Copyrites. Aboriginal Art in the Age of Reproductive Technologies*, Sydney: National Indigenous Arts Advocacy Association.

Kaiser, S. B, R. H. Nagasawa and S. S. Hutton (1991) 'Fashion, postmodernity and personal appearance: a symbolic interactionist formulation', *Symbolic Interaction*, 14:2, 165–85.

Kang, J. and K. Youn-Kyung (1998) 'Ethnicity and acculturation: influences on Asian American consumers' purchase decision making for social clothes', *Family and Consumer Sciences Research Journal*, 27:1 September. InfoTrac.

Kears, M. (1992) 'Natural collection', *Omni*, 14:9 June. InfoTrac.

Kegley Jnr., C. W. and E. R. Wittkopf (eds) (2001a) *The Global Agenda: Issues and Perspectives*, New York: McGraw Hill.

—— (2001b) *World Politics: Trend and Transformations* (8th edn), Boston: Bedford St Martins.

Kelley, R. (1997) 'Nap time: historicising the Afro', *Fashion Theory*, 1:4, 339–51.

Khan, N. (1992) 'Asian women's dress', in *Chic Thrills: A Fashion Reader*, eds. J. Ash and E. Wilson, London: Pandora Press, 61–74.

Klein, N. (2000) *No Logo*, London: Flamingo.

Klesse, C. (2000) 'Modern primitivism: non-mainstream body modification and racialized representation', in *Body Modification*, ed. M. Featherstone, London: Sage, 15–38.

Labrador, A. P. (1999) 'The project of nationalism: celebrating the centenary in Philippines contemporary art', *Humanities Research Bulletin*, 2, 53–70.

LaFeber, W. (1999) *Michael Jordan and the New Global Capitalism*, New York: W. W. Norton & Co.

Lash, S. (1999) *Another Modernity: A Different Rationality*, Oxford: Blackwells.

LeBlanc, M. N. (2000) 'Versioning womanhood and Muslimhood: fashion and the life course in contemporary Bouake, Cote d'Ivoire', *Africa*, 7:3, 442–81.

Lefebvre, H. (1991) *The Production of Space*, Oxford: Blackwells.

Lentz, C. (1995) 'Ethnic conflict and changing dress codes: a case study of an Indian migrant village in highland Ecuador', in *Dress and Ethnicity: Change Across Space and Time*, ed. J. B. Eicher, Oxford: Berg, 269–93.

Lindesfarne-Tapper, N. and B. Ingham (eds.) (1997) *Languages of Dress in the Middle East*, Richmond Surrey: Curzon Press.

Lipovetsky, G. (1994) *The Empire of Fashion: Dressing Modern Democracy*, trans. C. Porter, Princeton: Princeton University Press.

Li Xiaoping (1998) 'Fashioning the body in post-Mao China', *Consuming Fashion: Adorning the Transnational Body*, eds. A. Brydon and S. Neissen, Oxford: Berg, 71–90.

Lowe, M. and N. Wrigley (1996) 'Towards the new retail geography', *Retailing, Consumption and Capital: Toward the New Retail Geography*, Harlow, Essex: Longman Group, 3–30.

Lurie, A. (1992) *The Language of Clothes*, London: Bloomsbury Publications Ltd.

Lury, C. (1999) 'Marking time with Nike: the illusion of the durable', *Public Culture*, 11:3, 499–526.

Lynch, A. (1995) 'Hmong American New Year's dress: the display of ethnicity', *Dress and Ethnicity: Change Across Space and Time*, ed. J. B. Eicher, Oxford: Berg, 255–67.

McDonagh, M (1998) 'No style please we're on-message', *New Statesman*, 127, 25 September, InfoTrac.

McLaren, W. (1995) 'Wear it, write on it', *Object*, 3:4, 37–9.

MacMaster, N. and T. Lewis (1998) 'Orientalism: from unveiling to hyperveiling', *Journal of European Studies*, 28:1–2, 121–35.

McRobbie, A. (1988) 'Second-hand dresses and the role of the ragmarket', in *The Zoot Suits and Second-Hand Dresses: An Anthology of Fashion and Music*, ed. A. McRobbie, Boston: Unwin Hyman, 23–49.

Maffesoli, M. (1996) *The Times of the Tribes: The Decline of Individualism in Mass Society*, London: Sage.

Mandela. N. (1994) *Long Walk to Freedom*, London: Abacus Books.

Martin, R. (1992) 'T-shirt coda 1991', *Textile and Text*, 14:3, 27–9.

—— and H. Koda (1992a) 'T-Line: expressions of our time in the t-shirts of 1991', *Textile and Text*, 14:2, 13–17.

—— (1992b) 'V-O-T-E: the 1992 election in t-shirts', *Textile and Text*, 14: 3, 30–5.

Mathews, G. (2000) *Global Culture/Individual Identity: Searching for Home in the Cultural Supermarket*, London: Routledge.

Maynard, M. (2000a) 'Grassroots style: re-evaluating Australian fashion and Aboriginal art in the 1970s and 1980s', *Journal of Design History*, 13:2, 139–52.

—— (2000b) 'Griffith University's Tokyo vogue: couture at risk', *Eyeline*, 42, 19–21.

—— (2001) *Out of Line: Women and Style in Australia*, Sydney: New South Wales University Press.

—— (2002) 'Blankets: the visible politics of indigenous clothing in Australia', in *Fashioning the Body Politic*, ed. W. Parkins, Oxford: Berg, 189–204.

Mazrui, A. A. (1970) 'The robes of rebellion, sex, dress and politics in Africa', *Encounter*, 34, 19–30.

Meer, F. (1990) *Higher than Hope: The Authorised Biography of Nelson Mandela*, London: Penguin.

Miles, S. (1998) *Consumerism as a Way of Life*, London: Sage.

Miller, B. D. (1998) 'The disappearance of the oiled braid: Indian adolescent female hairstyles in North America', in *Hair: Its Power and Meaning in Asian Cultures*, eds. A. Hiltebeitel and B. D. Miller, Albany: State University of New York Press, 259–80.

Miller, D. (1995) 'Consumption as the vanguard of history', in *Acknowledging Consumption: A Review of New Studies*, ed. D. Miller, London: Routledge, 1–57.

—— (1998) *Shopping Place and Identity*, London: Routledge.

Molloy, J. T. (1975) *Dress for Success*, New York: Warner Books.

—— (1980) *Women: Dress for Success*, New York: Peter H. Wyden.

Molnar, A. K. (1998) 'Transformations in the use of traditional textiles of Ngada (Western Flores, Eastern Indonesia): commercialisation, fashion and ethnicity', in *Consuming Fashion: Adorning the Transnational Body*, eds. A. Brydon and S. Niessen, Oxford: Berg, 39–56.

Monga, E. D. (2000) 'Dollars and lipstick: the United States through the eyes of African women', *Africa*, 70:2, 192–208.

Moore, C. M., J. Fernie and S. Burt (2000) 'Brands without boundaries', *European Journal of Marketing*, 34: 8,. Business Source Premier.

Munoz, L. (2001) 'The suit is back – or is it? As dot-coms die so should business casual. But the numbers don't lie', *Fortune*, 143, 25 June. InfoTrac.

Mustafa, H. N. (1998) 'Sartorial ecumenes: African styles in a social and economic context', in *The Art of African Fashion*, eds. E. van der Plas and M. Willemsen, Eritrea: Africa World Press.

Nag, D. (1991) 'Fashion gender and the Bengali middle class', *Public Culture*, 3:2 Spring, 93–112.

Neville, R. (1996) *Hippie Hippie Shake: The Dreams, the Trips, the Trials, the Love-ins, the Screw ups … the Sixties*, Port Melbourne: Minerva.

Newton, J. (1988) 'Aborigines, tribes and the counterculture', *Social Analysis*, 23 August, 53–71.

Noble, G., S. Poynting and P. Taybar (1999) 'Youth ethnicity and the mapping of identities: strategic essentialism and strategic hybridity among male Arab-speaking youth in south-western Sydney', *Communal/Plural*, 7:1, 29–44.

Nordholt, H. S. (ed.) (1997) 'Introduction', in *Outward Appearances: Dressing State and Society in Indonesia*, Leiden: KITVL Press.

Norton, J. (1997) 'Faith and fashion in Turkey', in *Languages of Dress in the Middle East*, eds. N. Lindisfarne-Tapper and B. Ingham, Richmond Surrey: Curzon Press, 149–77.

Olivelle, P. (1998) 'Hair and society: social significance of hair in South Asian traditions', in *Hair: Its Power and Meaning in Asian Cultures*, eds, A. Hiltebeitel and B. D. Miller, Albany: State University of New York Press, 11–50.

O'Neal, G. S. (1999) 'The power of style: on rejection of the accepted', in *Appearance and Power*, eds. K. Johnson and S. Lennon, Oxford: Berg, 127–39.

Ophuls, W. and A. S. Boyan (1995) 'The international state of nature and the politics of scarcity', in *The Global Agenda: Issues and Perspectives*, eds. C. W. Kegley Jnr, and E. R. Wittkopf, New York: McGraw Hill, 436–45.

O'Rourke, P. J. (1998) 'The 1987 Reagan/Gorbachev Summit', in *Holidays in Hell*, London: Pan.

Parkins, Wendy (ed.) (2002) *Fashioning the Body Politic: Dress, Gender, Citizenship*, Oxford: Berg.

Perani, J. and N. H. Wolff (1999) *Cloth, Drapery and Patronage in Africa*, Oxford: Berg.

Perry, C. (1986) 'Op-shop fashion', *Time Out? Australian Left Review*, 98 Summer, 39–40.

Peters, M. and P. Roberts (1999) 'Globalisation and the crisis in the concept of the modern university', *Australian University Review*, 1, 47–55.

Philips Design (2000) *New Nomads. An Exploration of Wearable Electronics by Philips*, Rotterdam: 010 Publishers.

Polhemus, T. (1994) *Streetstyle. From Sidewalk to Catwalk*, London: Thames and Hudson.

—— (1998) *Deisel World Wide Wear*, London: Thames and Hudson.

Praveen, K., R. K. Aggarwal and P. Kumar (1994) 'Impact of industrial effluents on the soil and water quality of the desert ecosystem and its management', *Advances in Forestry Research in India*, 11, 79–104.

Puwar, N. (2002) 'Multicultural fashion ... stirrings of another sense of aesthetics and memory', *Feminist Review*, 71, 63–87.

Rasmussen, S. (1991–2) 'Veiled self: transparent meanings: Tuareg headdress as social expression', *Ethnology*, 30–1, 101–17.

Ray, L. and A. Sayer (eds.) (1999) *Culture and Economy After the Cultural Turn*, London: Sage.

Robins, K. (1991) 'Tradition and translation: national culture and its global context', in *Enterprise and Heritage: Crosscurrents of National Culture*, eds. J. Corner and S. Harvey, London: Routledge, 21–44.

Robinson, F. (1993) *The Man in the Bowler Hat: His History and Iconography*, Chapel Hill: University of North Carolina Press.

Roe, J. (1997–8) 'Dayspring: Australia and New Zealand as a setting for the "New Age", from the 1980s to Nimbin', *Australian Cultural History*, 16, 170–87.

Rojek, C. and J. Urry (eds.) (1997) *Touring Cultures: Transformation of Travel and Theory*, New York: Routledge.

Rosenblatt, D. (1997) 'The antisocial skin: structure, resistance, and "Modern Primitive" adornment in the United States', *Cultural Anthropology*, 12:3, 287–334.

Ross, A. (1994) 'Tribalism in effect', in *On Fashion*, eds. S. Benstock and S. Ferriss, Brunswick New Jersey: Rutgers University Press, 284–99.

Ryan, M. (1996) 'Is dry cleaning all wet?', *World Watch*, 6:3 May–June. InfoTrac.

Sayer, C. (1985) *Mexican Costume*, London: British Museum.

Schoss, J. (1996) 'Dressed to "shine": work, leisure, and style in Malindi, Kenya', in *Clothing and Difference: Embodied Identities in Colonial and Post-Colonial Africa*, ed. H. Hendrickson, Durham: Duke University Press, 157–88.

Schouten, G. (1999) 'South Africa: just a change of clothes', *Radio Netherlands: World Hot Spots*, 15 June, www.vnw.nl/hotspots/archive/zaf/html/southafrica150699.html.

Sekimoto, T. (1997) 'Uniforms and concrete walls: dressing the village under the New Order in the 1970s and 1980s', in *Outward Appearances: Dressing State and Society in Indonesia*, ed. H. S. Nordholt, Leiden: KITLV Press, 307–38.

Seng, Y. J. and B. Wass (1995) 'Traditional Palestinian wedding dress as a symbol of nationalism', in *Dress and Ethnicity: Change Across Space and Time*, ed. J. B. Eicher, Oxford: Berg, 227–54.

Sennett, R. (1977) *The Fall of Public Man*, New York: Alfred Knopf.

Soh, C. H. (1992) 'Skirts, trousers or hanbok? The politics of image making among Korean women legislators', *Women's Studies International Forum*, 15:3, 375–84.

Solomon, R. C. (1991) 'Business ethics', in *A Companion to Ethics*, ed. P. Singer, Oxford: Blackwells, 354–65.

Soroos, M. S. (2001) 'The tragedy of the commons in global perspective', in *The Global Agenda: Issues and Perspectives*, eds. C. W. Kegley Jr and E. R. Wittkopf, New York: McGraw Hill, 483–97.

Sowell, T. (1994) *Race and Culture: A World View*, New York: Basic Books.

Spring, C. and J. Hudson (1995) *North African Textiles*, London: British Museum.

Sprout, H. and M. (1971) *Towards a Politics of Planet Earth*, Princeton: Van Nostrand-Reinhold for the Centre of International Studies.

Swiss, T. (2000) 'Leather substitutes resource guide', http://unreasonable.org/vegan/leather-substitutes.html, 20 April (accessed August 2000).

Szerszynski, B. (1999) 'Performing politics', in *Culture and Economy After the Cultural Turn*, eds. L. Ray and A. Sayer, London: Sage, 211–28.

Tarlo, E. (1996) *Clothing Matters: Dress and Identity in India*, London: Hurst and Company.

Taylor, L. (2000) 'The Hilfiger factor and the flexible commercial world of couture', in *The Fashion Business*, eds. N. White and I. Griffiths, Oxford: Berg, 121–42.

—— (2002) *The Study of Dress History*, Manchester: Manchester University Press.

Thomas, N. (1991) *Entangled Objects: Exchange, Material Culture and Colonialism in the Pacific*, Cambridge Massachusetts: Harvard University Press.

Thomas, S. and M. Arora (2000) 'Tokyo v London', *The Face*, September, 204–10.

Torgovnick, M. (1990) *Gone Primitive: Savage Intellects, Modern Lives*, Chicago: University of Chicago Press.

van Dijk, K. (1997) 'Sarong, jubbah, and trousers: appearance as a means of distinction and discrimination', in *Outward Appearances: Dressing State and Society in Indonesia*, ed. H. S. Nordholt, Leiden: KITLV Press.

Veblen, T. (1934) *The Theory of the Leisure Class*, New York: Modern Library, 1934 edition.

Virilio, P. (1994) *The Vision Machine*, Bloomington: Indiana University Press.

Wagner, S. A. (1997) *Understanding Green Consumer Behaviour: A Qualitative Cognitive Approach*, London: Routledge.

Warwick, A. and D. Cavallaro (1998) *Fashioning the Frame: Boundaries Dress and the Body*, Oxford: Berg.

Wassmann, J. (ed.) (1998) *Pacific Answers to Western Hegemony: Cultural Practices of Identity Construction*, Oxford: Berg.

Watson, L. (1988) 'The Commonwealth Games in Brisbane: analysis of Aboriginal protests', *Social Alternatives*, 7:1, 37–43.

Weiss, B. (1996) 'Dressing at death: clothing, time, and memory in Buhaya, Tanzania', in *Clothing and Difference: Embodied Identities in Colonial and Post-Colonial Africa*, ed. H. Hendrickson, Durham: Duke University Press, 133–54.

Wilson, E. (1985) *Adorned in Dreams: Fashion and Modernity*, London: Virago.

—— and L. Taylor (1989) *Through the Looking Glass: A History of Dress from 1860 to the Present Day*, London: BBC Books.

Wood, R. E. (1998) 'Tourist ethnicity: a brief itinerary', *Ethnic and Racial Studies*, 21:2 March, 218–41.

Yamani, M. (1997) 'Changing the habits of a lifetime: the adaptation of Hejazi dress to the new social order', *Languages of Dress in the Middle East*, eds. N. Lindesfarne-Tapper and B. Ingham, Richmond Surrey: Curzon Press, 55–66.

York, P. (1999) 'A serious dressing down: management today', July. InfoTrac.

Yunfeng, L. (1999) 'Chinese fashion traditions catch on worldwide', June. InfoTrac.

Zuhur, Z. (2001) 'The mixed impact of feminist struggles in Egypt during the 1990s', *Meria: Middle East Journal of International Affairs*, 5:1 March. InfoTrac.

Newspaper/magazine articles (authored)

Dunstan, G. (1978) 'Pathways to wholeness', *Nimbin News*, 16 October.

Edgecliffe-Johnson, A. (2000) 'Tightening Levis belt', *Financial Times*, 28 February.

Farrell, S. (2001) 'In fear of the Taliban's mark of the unbeliever', *Australian*, 24 May.

Hamilton, K. and K. Martineau (1997) 'Future fashions are not quite ready to wear', *Newsweek*, 4 August. InfoTrac.

Jackson, D. (2001) 'Sneaky feelings', *Australian*, 17 August.

Jackson, S. (2002) 'A unifying thread runs through Kazai's outfit', *Weekend Australian*, 2–3 February.

Kay, K. (2002) 'Top pilot sues to unveil a cover-up', *Australian*, 9 January.

Lindblad, J. (1976a) 'Where the drop-outs are', *Bulletin*, 98:5000, 27 March.

—— (1976b) 'Dropping-out: how to avoid the pitfalls', *Bulletin*, 3 April.

Lunn, S. (2001a) 'Change and a groovy haircut in the wind', *Australian*, 24 April.

—— (2001b) 'Swept in on a maverick wave', *Australian*, 26 April.

Lyall, K. (2002) 'Muslim pupils banned for headscarves', *Australian*, 6 February.

McIntyre, P. (2001) 'Bursting the global bubble', *Australian* (Media) 2–8 August.

Mofokeng, L. (1999) 'He made Madiba shirts a cut above the rest', *Sunday Times*, 11 July, www.sundaytimes.co.za/1999/07/11arts/gauteng/aneg07.htm.

O'Sullivan, J. (2001) 'Voices behind the veil', *Guardian*, 24 September.

Owens, S. (1993) 'Colouring up the Japanese market', *Sun Herald*, 20 June.

Peek, L. (2001) 'Female top gun takes aim at Saudi dress code', *Australian*, 20 April.

Ryle, J. (2000) 'Miracles of the sacred grove', *Times Literary Supplement*, 21 April.

Symonds, S. (1990) 'Earth wear', *Sydney Morning Herald Good Living Supplement*, 24 July.

Wynhausen, E. (2001) 'Shock of the new left', *Australian*, 26 September.

Newspaper/magazine articles (unauthored)

Africa News Service (1999) 'He's got Africa in his blood', 23 September. InfoTrac.

Australian (2001) 'Bullet enforces dress code', 15–16 September.

Business Week (1999) 'Sweatshop reform: how to solve the standoff', 3 May. InfoTrac.

East African Weekly (1998) 'Not suitable for Tanzania?', 19–25 October. www.nation-audio.com/News/EastAfrican/1910/Opinion/Opinion10.html.

The Economist (2000) 'Natural style', 3 June. InfoTrac.

Observer Magazine (1999) London, 11 April.

Peoples Weekly (1993) 'The year in Hillary', 25 October. InfoTrac.

Reports

Patterns of Textile, Clothing and Footwear Trade within APEC 1990–94 (1997). Report for Productivity Commission, Commonwealth of Australia, Canberra.

'The Global 2000 Report to the President: Entering the 21st Century' (1980) A report by the Council of Environmental Quality and the Department of State, New York: Pergamon.

Index

St. Louis Community College
at Meramec
LIBRARY